M. Laura Crescimanno

CHARMING SICILY

itineraries, resorts and useful suggestions

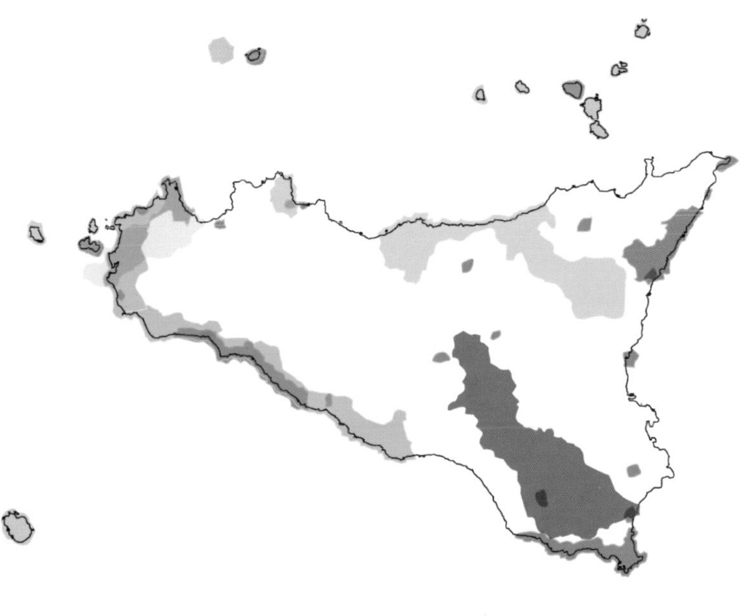

MCe
Marcello Clausi Editore

M. Laura Crescimanno
CHARMING SICILY

Palermo - Italy
ISBN: 978-88-903815-4-6

EDITORIAL COORDINATOR
Claudia Mirto

ILLUSTRATED BY
Alfio Garozzo

DESIGNED BY
Vincenzo Vuono

TRANSLATED BY
Ivana Mannino

ACKNOWLEDGEMENTS:
Marine Superintendency of the region of Sicily
Photoreport archives and Public Relations Office,
Alta Marea Diving, Marettimo Diving

Special thanks for tourist information:
Antonio Condorelli, Elena Di Dio,
Max Firreri, Gaetano Guzzardo,
Franz La Paglia, Giuseppe Martorana,
Josè Trovato

Publisher:
MC
Marcello Clausi Editore
Viale delle Alpi 56
90144 Palermo - Italy
Tel. +39 091329181

WWW.CLAUSIEDITORE.IT
WWW.SUGGESTIONIDISICILIA.IT

Printed in June 2010 by Officine Grafiche Riunite

INTRODUCTION

A CHARMING JOURNEY, THE WAY YOU LIKE IT

Sicily is wide and various. It is a real kaleidoscope of places, realities and landscapes that change every month thanks to a mild weather and a changeable light, in a word, Mediterranean.
The idea of this publication starts from my wish to gather plenty of notes, addresses and trip suggestions that I collected during my wandering through the island in order to carry out tour reports and reportages. Putting them down in black and white instead of dictating them to my friends by phone or via mail. It also starts from a statement of fact that the time at disposal for those who travel is never enough, it is useful, therefore, having practical advice by someone who has lived the same experience.
So here are ten thematic chapters, including some pictures made by Alfio Garozzo, where the only thread running through is to let the reader find out a new Sicily.
This is the best I have seen and selected, mentioning each time a stopover you cannot miss, a tasty dish, a museum, a landscape, a path, a hotel on the beach, a peaceful shore and even a seabed where to plunge. The beauty of a journey the way you like.
You can walk through the old town, with its new multi-ethnic aspect, then leave by car from Palermo, and drive along the most charming itinerary towards east or west or create a series of routes depending on the time at your disposal.
Obviously you are not going to find here all the Sicily tour but detailed options to travel over cities, suburbs, countrysides, shores and minor islands. This is not a classic guidebook but a suggestion of ten mini-journeys off the course of mass tourism. You will find tips on small hotels, big events, new resorts, holiday farms and B&B in the old town, unmissable restaurants, wines to taste and sea bathing you cannot forget. The new and, I hope, the best of the Sicilian hospitality to find out a thousand islands that form the main one.
I want to thank the publisher that believed in my idea, the author of the pictures, the staff for the patient editorial work, the graphic designer that supported me in the difficult selection of pictures and subjects, and all the people who provided me with images and advice.

M. Laura Crescimanno

CONTENTS

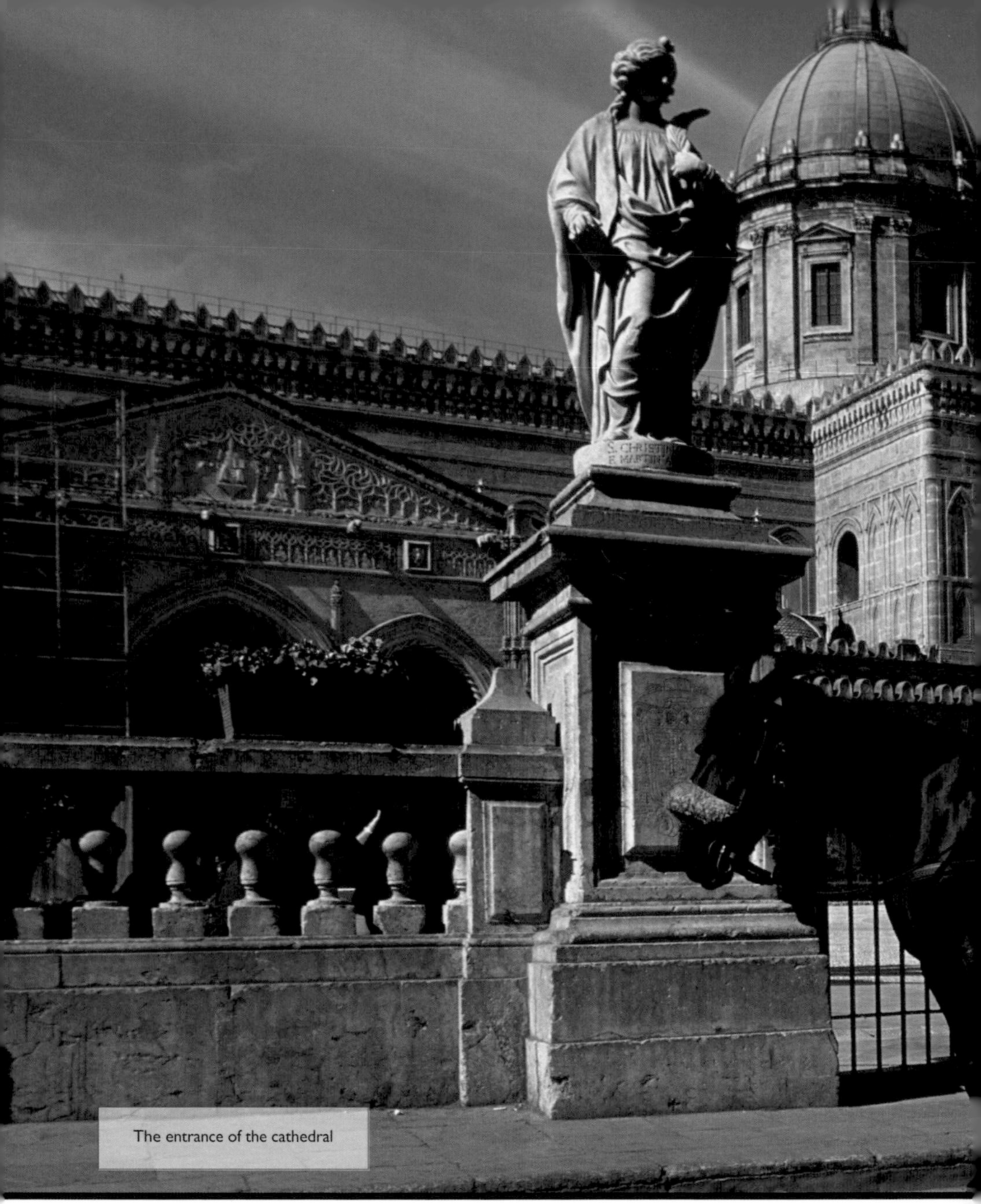

The entrance of the cathedral

01

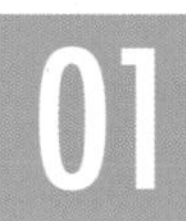

A WALK IN THE **OLD TOWN**

Palermo is a multiethnic city with a lot of souls melt as one, souls that live together in the local cooking, in the dialect, in the historic market places, in the Norman-Arab architecture, in the baroque facades, even in the tropical gardens and in the buildings that recall The Leopard novel that are opening again

The oldest building of the city is the local Parliament. It includes the district of Palazzo Reale; the other three districts of the old town were Monte di Pietà, Castellammare and Tribunali. Discovering the old town by walking along means sinking into the contrasts of the history, the mosaic of the cultures and arts that seal the heart of Palermo and its inhabitants and seduces its visitors.

Start from the Palatine Chapel, carried out by king Roger in 1130 and considered today as the unique proof of the Norman-Arab mosaic in its original splendour that you can visit also at night. (Fondazione Federico II, Tel. 0916256013).

Leaving the palm grove of piazza Vittoria, on the left, you can go towards a district called Papireto. There, one of the two rivers, that together with the Kemonia crossed the Arab city, used to flow. Behind the cathedral you can stop in the quiet and small piazza Sett'Angeli in order to admire the big apses of the Norman-Arab monument where an incredible overlapping of architectural styles testify the presence of plenty of civilizations in the old Panormus over the centuries.

And now Corso Vittorio Emanuele, also called Cassaro of the Arab Al Quasar (Fortress) with the Spanish facades with the over-elabo-

A SITE
YOU CANNOT MISS

The Cathedral

It was built by the middle of the twelfth century, frequently restored until the 18th-century interventions. This mighty building stands on a garden surrounded by baroque style walls; two towers with double lancet window and the impressive 16th-century portal with Gothic figures dominate it. The Norman apsidal front shows geometric and animal patterns of great value. The severe lines of the interior belong to the late 18th-century. In the chapel on the right you can find the imperial tombs of Frederick II, his wife Constance of Aragon, Roger II and his daughter, the empress Constance. The silver cinerary urn containing the relics of the patroness Santa Rosalia is kept in the interior.

Above, Piazza Pretoria, next to it, a view of the archbishop's palace, on the left, the Quattro Canti

rate baroque buildings, the ceramic and souvenirs shops in the courts, the old second-hand book sellers, the hotels, the B&B that are increasingly opening in the aristocratic residences of the old town. During the day it is a big bazaar throbbing with life swarming with young students, residents, non-EU citizens and tourists; at night, it becomes a more and more busy route. On the left, on the Montevergini alley, there is a deconsecrated church with a monastery that in the last few years have become a night stopover for shows, music, literary cafés, meeting places and wine bars.
Walking down towards the Cassaro, on your right, you can see the historic square called piazza Bologni with the statue of Charles V that stretches its arm towards the new contemporary art gallery in the Palazzo Belmonte Riso. A few metres from the Centrale Palace Hotel, with its beautiful high-terraced restaurant and its view over the roofs of the old town, there is a first example of the several baroque treasures of the city: the San Salvatore Oratory in its octagonal plan, with the wonderful stuccowork by Serpotta. Still walking, you can see another example of

The Capo Market, a detail of the market stalls full of dried fruit and legumes, on the right a typical booth selling canned fish, sardines, anchovies and salted herrings

the baroque opulence that is the Church of San Giuseppe dei Teatini. This building of the 1612 is very impressive because of the contrast of the austerity of the late Renaissance style in the outside.

The Quattro Canti area, also called piazza Vigliena, full expression of the Spanish influence of the early 17th century, was considered as a meeting place within the four districts. By looking upwards, you can see three different pictures: the four seasons, the four Spanish viceroys and the four patronesses of the city.

On your right, very impressive is the marble view of the fountain in piazza Pretoria surrounded by the facades of buildings and churches. Very lighted is Palazzo dell Aquile, seat of the Municipality. Behind this building you can see the symbol of the city: the red domes of Santa Maria dell'Ammiraglio, also called Martorana, that overlooks the steps and the entrance of the spectacular baroque Church of Santa Caterina. You cannot miss the representation of the Sepulchre. In the same square, the historical pizzeria Bellini stands together with the recently opened small theatre. Not far from there, you can see other treasures of the Palermo baroque style; walking towards via del Ponticello

OTHER HISTORIC MARKETS

In order to experience the Arab spirit of the "grascia" (filth in Sicilian dialect) of the market places of Palermo, between decline and revival, folklore and daily nature, a must-stop is the Vucciria, popular set of the painting by Guttuso shown at Palazzo Chiaramonte Steri.

The Capo, beyond the Teatro Massimo, is a different world. It is protected by Porta Carini, old defensive bastion that meet via Volturno along the walls of the old town of Palermo. You better go early in the morning when the plentiful and tidy goods, placed under the lights and coloured tents, are a real scenery; several shops also work half day on Wednesdays. People go to the Capo in order to buy very fresh fish that the Nuccio family has sold for over 50 years. It is the first fishmonger on the right, but not the only one, that

BESIDES **VUCCIRIA, CAPO AND BALLARÒ**

testifies the variety of the Mediterranean with huge gropers, swordfish, amberjacks, giltheads, large shrimps, crayfish and lobsters. There are amazing booths selling fruit and vegetables: very scented basil, parsley, fennel and mint all gathered together in huge bunches, it looks like a party of colours and perfumes. Around lunchtime, some professionals working in the area (the market place is near the Law Courts) go there in order to taste the local delights, very good are the ones of Danotti brothers, big arancine*[1] filled with butter or meat, pane and panelle, sfincione, fried and filled aubergines, pasta with anchovies, that you can find in the typical fast food of Palermo called rosticceria.
The market place has lived a revival for about one year also thanks to the reopening, after fifteen years, of the Church Immacolata Concezione. It is a spectacular church for its polychromic marble altars, open on Sunday for the 12 a.m. Holy Mass.
Further on, instead of the old Archetto wine shop, a very elegant small restaurant called "Sopra i mura" stands today. Another thing you cannot miss is the liberty facade of the oldest baker's of the district decorated with a coloured mosaic. You can find it beyond the square of the Capo turning on the right towards via Cappuccinelle.
From via Maqueda you can get to the market Ballarò by following the road signs beyond the Quattro Canti that bring to the Arab alleys on the right. This is the multiethnic Palermo, it is almost a souk. Tunisians, Filipinos, Tamils and Central Africans that live in the district usually shop at the market that in the last few years has brought Asian goods. Starting from the square of Ballarò, among the oldest shops, you cannot miss the one that sells dried fruit, legumes of different colours, pineapples, mangos, papaw, dried apricots, varied spice, cinnamon, liquorice, pistachios from Bronte (town of Sicily in the province of Catania), hazelnuts, dried figs, dates etc. arranged in small baskets. It is a real joy for your eyes and your nose. If you walk on, beyond the big booths that sell meat you can still eat a broth made with all the parts of the beef and the "quarume" that is the boiled interiors to eat standing up surrounded by the crowd and the noisy voices of the street vendors. Walking through the booths selling fruits and vegetables you can get to the square dominated by the Church of the Carmine. From dawn to dusk you can find booths selling fish and vegetables, olives coming from all over the Mediterranean, salty and canned fish. The market closes at 1 p.m. on Sundays.

on the opposite side of via Maqueda, next to the city library, you can see Casa Professa, the imposing house or Church of the Holy name of Jesus built by Jesuits in 1564. The entrance is on a big court; it is a heaven of peace among the old walls while on the outside the second-hand market stalls rejoin the Ballarò market in one single swarming souk. At night, among the alleys, small pubs and jazz clubs like the fashionable Gatto Nero are open. There, the new talents of the Sicilian jazz meet to play.

From the Quattro Canti to the Teatro Massimo

Walking down via Maqueda towards the new city enjoy a quick peep at the alleys on the left. During the day they are brimming with goods and at night livened up by the new pubs where you can have dinner or a drink outdoor.
Once you get past piazza Sant'Onofrio, walking through via dei Giovenchi, you will find the historic square of Beati Paoli, where, with the help of a tour guide, it is possible to walk down along the underground passages that used to bring to the well-known sect of Palermo.
In the middle of the square you can see the characteristic refreshment

*1 Fried rice balls coated with breadcrumbs originated in Sicily in the 10th century.

A SITE YOU CANNOT MISS

The Castle of Zisa

El aziz from the Arabian means the splendid and is the seat of the Islamic art museum. It testifies the magnificence of the Norman-Arab period.
The park, which once was destined to royal amusements, was recently opened for summer concerts. It shows the architecture of the Arabian garden with marbled paths and waterfalls surrounded by green spaces. It was built around 1160 for William I, today it seems to be swallowed by the chaos of the northern districts of the city. The square ground-floor room is rich in mosaics with hunting figures and an Arabian spring. Upstairs, there are other sitting rooms while on the sides you can find the six royal apartments.

booths where you can taste juices and citrus fruit squashes. Late in the afternoon, the busiest street for young people is via dei Candelai. There, surrounded by the smell of African spice you can find Maghreb pubs where you can eat the kebab. The first one to open was I Candelai with a pop and dark atmosphere and live international music. You are almost behind piazza Verdi where the great liberty scene dominates, at the crossroads with via Ruggero Settimo that is the modern major road of the city.
In front of the theatre there is the small street via Bara all'Olivella, livened up by small clubs and crafts, ceramic and jewels shops. This is the kingdom of Mimmo Cuticchio, brilliant successor of the tradition of the Sicilian puppet-master with his atelier and puppet theatre. Going towards piazza Olivella you can see the baroque facade of the Salinas museum and the Church of Sant'Ignazio, then walking on the back of the Post Office building you can reach piazza San Domenico also known as the Pantheon of the noble Sicilian people with its 18th-century big facade overlooking the baroque column with the Virgin on the top.
Behind the big square, you can admire the late 16th-century oratory of Santa Cita in via Valverde, the SS. Rosario of San Domenico in via dei

A panoramic picture of the gulf and the domes of the old town seen from the terrace Montevergini, on the right the fountain of Piazza Pretoria

01

A SITE
YOU CANNOT MISS

Teatro Massimo

It is considered as the symbol of the recovered culture, monument of the liberty style and temple of the lyric; it is one of the biggest theatres of Europe, the second after the Opera of Paris and renowned for the excellent acoustic. It was built in a neoclassical style by the architects Ernesto and Filippo Basile and shows in the front the emblematic expression "L'arte rinnova i popoli e ne rivela la vita" (Art renews the people and reveals life to them). Impressive is the metal liberty-style dome, the big staircase of the front lined with the statues of the Lyric and the Tragedy by Mario Rutelli. The foyer and the interior are open to the public; it is one of the few theatres to have a summer seat, the Teatro di Verdura.
Tel. 0916090831 - 800907080
Opening: from Tue to Sun 10.30 a.m. to 2.30 p.m.

The imposing steps of the entrance of the Teatro Massimo, temple of the Liberty style, in the picture below on the right Porta Felice, gateway to the promenade

Bambinai with the stuccowork by the sculptor Serpotta. If you stop for a moment in piazza San Domenico, before you walk along the alleys that bring to the Vucciria market and go on until corso Vittorio Emanuele, you could stop and taste the fine food of the small restaurant Sant'Andrea (Tel. 091334999).
Deafened by the atmosphere of the market, take a nostalgic look at the old small restaurant Shangai situated in the same square of the market, where the inhabitants of Palermo still go to buy great fish: from this windows Guttuso painted his famous picture.
Spring out again at the Cassaro and keep going towards the Marina among the art shops, traditional crafts and old grocery stores. Before plunging in the swarming piazza Marina, visit the Emporio of Pizzo Free at the street number 172; you cannot miss the pane e panelle*2 at the fried-food place Francu u vastiddaru.

***2** Sicilian fritters made from chickpea flour. They are a popular street food in Palermo and are often eaten between bread or on a roll, like a sandwich.

MUSEUMS YOU CANNOT MISS

Palazzo Abatellis

Few steps beyond the Marina, with its impressive facade decorated with triple lanced window, the Palazzo Abatellis was built in 1495 in the late Gothic-Catalan style and completely restored in the 1960s by Carlo Scarpa. It still keeps in the interior art collections from the Middle Ages to the thirteenth-century. Beyond the courtyard with the open gallery you can walk upstairs. On the second floor you can see the renowned fifteenth-century fresco "Il trionfo della morte" (the triumph of death), strong allegory of the plague and the death in Palermo. In the next rooms you can find wooden and marble sculptures from the fourth to the sixteenth century by the Gagini's school. The X room is fully dedicated to the Annunziata by Antonello Da Messina.

Address: via Alloro, 4
Tel. 091623001!
Opening: 9 a.m. to I p.m. / 2.30 to 7 p.m.

Salinas archaeological museum

From 1866, the former monastery of Filipinos keeps valuable finds of Selinunte on the ground floor. In the cloister near the entrance with its sixteenth-century fountain and in the adjacent rooms you can find decorated anchor stocks and Punic, Greek and Roman anchors, all underwater archaeology materials coming from the Western Sicily. And still, Punic and Egyptian items, woman's marble sarcophaguses, a Punic godhead to the throne, Egyptian statues and inscriptions. In the main cloister you can find Roman statues and relieves of Sicilian origin and Greek inscriptions coming from the temples of Selinunte.

Address: piazza Olivella, 24
Tel. 0916116805
Opening: 8.30 am to 6.45 p.m. from Mon to Sat
9 a.m. to 1.30 p.m. Sundays and holiday

From the Kalsa to the Marina

This is one of the most interesting and dynamic places of the city. During the summer and weekends it is livened up by the cultural life until night, on Sunday mornings by a noisy market that sells old curiosity and collector's items.

Among the facades of the buildings, Villa Garibaldi stands out in the middle with its spectacular crown of the huge ficus leaning forward Palazzo Chiaramonte Steri. On the right side of the square there is via Lungarini, with the entrance of Palazzo Mirto that today is the regional museum and wonderful example of life and habits of the Palermo of the 18th-century. If you take via Merlo, you can get to the back of the wonderful piazzetta San Francesco, dominated by the Renaissance facade of the 13th-century church that contains precious works of art. You cannot miss a stopover to the old Focacceria San Francesco, the oldest focacceria of the city filled with tables in a Liberty style room. There, you can taste the insuperable sfincione[*3] and the "pane con la meusa" (bread filled with beef spleen). During summer, the square is full of tables in order to have

*3 Variety of sliced pizza originated in Palermo where the cheese is mixed with the tomato sauce, anchovies and onions.

The new street furniture of the Marina promenade called "green sea" by the inhabitants of Palermo

open-air dinners or a Sicilian wine tasting in the nearest wine bar called "Mi manda Picone".

By taking via Alloro, towards the sea, you can get to a district called Kalsa. Among the dark alleys and the under-restoration buildings rescued from the last war, you can get to piazza Magione. On the right side there is the very old basilica Magione and walking down via dello Spasimo you can reach instead all the remains of the garden and the deconsecrated church of Santa Maria dello Spasimo, always open for concerts and exhibitions. Further on, beyond the Oratorio dei Bianchi you can find the beautiful piazza Kalsa framed by the Palazzo De Seta and dominated by the baroque facade of the Church of Santa Teresa, covered with lights during the summer. This is the heart of the Arab Palermo livened up by concerts and open-air theatres during the summer.

By taking via Torremuzza and then via Butera you can notice again the contrast between the historic aristocratic buildings like the Crutched Friar, the houses of the noble families Alliata, Butera and Lanza and the small folk wine-shops. You can stop at the small theatre Ditirammu with its Sicilian puppet-master workroom that hosts performances and exhibitions on the folk theatre of Palermo. If you go back towards the sea, by walking down the monumental Porta Felice, background of the Festino di

BAROQUE ITINERARY AMONG CHURCHES, ORATORIES AND NEW PUBS

In the old town, you cannot miss a full immersion in the baroque style of the Serpotta's family, sculptor masters that gave to the stuccoes and the stones the incredible movement and the grace of living things by following the style of Serpotta in the itineraries mapped out by the Municipality.
There is a well-known Serpotta for the tourists that love art, and a hidden Serpotta, the one to be discovered beyond walls and gates or in the corners of magnificent churches where the baroque style is a celebration of the opulence.
The itinerary goes to the Oratorio dei Bianchi, Santa Maria della Pietà, the Immacolatella, the Church of Sant'Agostino, the Oratories of SS Rosario in San Domenico and Santa Cita, just to name a few (the churches are open in the morning or by appointment, info www.comunepa.it, www.amicimuseisiciliani.it).
Between a church and an oratory, walking along corso Vittorio, cut in half by the set of the Quattro Canti, among the alleys, you can strike out into an Arabian maze of markets and shops. Going so far as a walk on the beach, you cannot miss a drink, good music and a library open late into the evening, the Kalhesa Kursaal, (Foro Umberto 21) next to the popular ice-cream shop "da Ilardo". A quieter literary walk can be done in via Alloro, near piazza Marina, at the back of the Foro Italico (big green area that spreads on the seaside of Palermo) ad the new garden on the sea.
In order to have an open-air appetizer among the stirs of The Leopard novel you can go to the Caffé Letterario in vicolo della Neve all'Alloro, named after the prince of Lampedusa. It shows clothes and antiques taken from the movie. You can also go to Expà in via Alloro, where you can enjoy appetizers, music and architecture exhibitions and other arts, or to Mikalsa to make a selection of foreign biers and live music in the lively and folksy district called Kalsa.

Santa Rosalia[*4], you could end up doing the famous walk on a carriage, very popular tradition during the belle époque period where the renowned small orchestra used to play outdoor on Sundays. In the first weeks of July, the walk on the seaside becomes a real celebration in honour of the patroness of Palermo. It is a popular explosion of the sacred and the profane that ends up on the night of the July 14, with the crossing of the carriage and pair and the usual fireworks. You can walk around from one side under the shadow of the building's walls or to the other side towards the new open-air lawn on the seaside. By walking, you can get to the nature reserve of Villa Giulia and Orto Botanico (botanical garden). Further on, at Sant'Erasmo, you can find the new contemporary art exhibition area, big shed that used to be a deposit of railway engines situated between the sea and the mouth of the river Oreto.

From the Cala to Mondello

Exhausted from the city crush let's plunge now into the nature. After you visit the just-opened archaeological site of Castello a Mare, the Arab bastion, guard of the old city that in the summer becomes a meeting-place with music, at the Cala take the car and drive along towards Mount Pellegrino and Mondello. Walk up on the so loved mount; a panoramic street climbs up towards Castello Utveggio and the Sanctuary of Santa Rosalia. From there, after you go through a valley of wood, you can get down towards the gulf of Mondello. To get to the beach, seven kilometres away,

***4** Religious and traditional procession of the holy carriage of the Saint held in the old town each year on July 15 for the celebration of St. Rosalia.

MONREALE AMONG ALLEYS AND MOSAICS

The Archbishop's palace can be reached by car going towards corso Calatafimi after 7 km from the city centre. Once you get to piazza Vittorio Emanuele you can see the impressive massive structure of the cathedral, built by William I between 1172 and 1176. The big bronze portal and the two bell towers are very impressive. Also wonderful are the apses decorated with dead arches, they stand on the oldest district of the city called Ciambra. Here, in the Palazzo dei Principi of Cutò situated in largo Cutò you can spend the night in a B&B with a view on the apses. The dome reveals its magnificence in the interior. The walls are fully covered with wonderful polychromatic and pure gold mosaics that portray some scenes of the Bible and spread for six thousand and three hundred square metres. The perspective culminates in the Chorus with the magnificent image of Pantocrator Christ. It is twelve metres tall and visible from any side. The right side contains the mausoleum with the remains of William II the Good and William I the Bad. On the left nave there is the entrance to the treasure with valuable goldsmith and sacred art manufactured articles. From piazza Guglielmo, a must-see is the Cloister with its well-known 114 couples of mosaic columns and the walk on the roof from where you can enjoy the panoramic view on the entire valley called Conca d'Oro. The entrance is inside the church. Next to the dome, you can see the monumental complex of William II. Seat of The Civic Gallery that hosts the eighteenth-century painting by Novelli and Velasco, it is characterized by wonderful bright rooms. Once you pass the big hall you can enter the elegant lookout, previously farmed by the monks and now full of ancient ficus. Here you can admire another earthenware statuesque by Gagini representing the Holy Family.

Walking along the streets of the city centre you cannot miss the Balsano baker's called L'antica Forneria Tusa placed in via Odigitria on the back of the dome. There, you can try the popular wood-burning bread and the biscuits covered with sugary icing. Towards via Torres, before you get to the city car park, you will find the shops of the mosaic craftwork.

Opening of the Cathedral and the Treasure: Mon to Sun 8 a.m. to 6.30 p.m. in summer
8 to 12.30 a.m. – 3.30 to 6.30 p.m. in winter
Cloister: Mon to Sat 9 am to 7 p.m.
Complex: Mon to Sat 8 a.m. to 7 p.m.

On the left, the Dome of Monreale, Above, the Charleston bathing establishment along the beach of Mondello

you can choose different solutions: you can cross the park of Favorita, full of paths and old vegetable gardens and citrus orchards, drive along the mount crossing the seaside small villages Vergine Maria, Acquasanta and Arenella, or choose the street towards Tommaso Natale in order to admire some of the villas where the aristocratic inhabitants of Palermo used to spend the rich and idle summer holidays. A must-see is Villa Niscemi, luxury seat of the Municipality and the Palazzina Cinese that has just been restored. The equipped beach, with several accessible passages open to the public, is very crowded during the summer but quiet and with tropical colours in the mild days of autumn and winter. In the square you can find typical Sicilian food, seafood, great ice cream and the restored Tower of Tonnara, open to the public.
The promontory of Mount Pellegrino, watershed between the gulf of Palermo and the gulf of Mondello, was well loved by Goethe that in his trip to Sicily called it "the most beautiful gulf of the world". On the top of the mountain you can find the sanctuary of Santa Rosalia, patroness of Palermo, wonderful place both for the natives and the past travellers. In September 4, both the worshippers and atheists go on a pilgrimage to ask for a blessing, a gift or just a small favour by walking through an old paved street that starts from the slope of the mountain. Once, you could

THE PALACES OF CULTURE

Palazzo Ziino
Address: via Dante, 53
Tel. 0917407631
It is a beautiful 20th-century building. On the first floor you can find the exhibition area, the plaster casts gallery and a collection of 64 plaster sculptures. On the second floor, Contemporary Art exhibitions, on the third floor the media library. Opening of the exhibitions: from Tue to Sun 9 a.m. to 7.30 p.m. The media library is open from Mon to Sat 9.30 a.m. to 6.30 p.m.

Palazzo Belmonte Riso
Address: corso V. Emanuele, 365
Tel. 091320532
Seat of the Contemporary Art Museum of Sicily, it was built at the end of the eighteenth century in baroque and neoclassical style. Open from Tue to Sun 10 a.m. to 7 p.m. Fry and Sun till 10 p.m.

Palazzo Sant'Elia
Address: via Maqueda, 81
Tel. 0916628111
Considered as one of the most sumptuous buildings of the city because of its dimension, facade and frescos, it was restored in the eighteenth century by the Municipality and it is now seat of international temporary exhibitions. Open from Mon to Sun 9 a.m. to 8 p.m. during exhibitions.

Villa Zito Museo Mormino
Address: via Libertà, 52
Tel. 091608597I
It shows collections of paintings and majolica objects.
Open from Mon to Fry 9 a.m. to 1 p.m. and 3 to 5 p.m. Sat 9 a.m. to 1 p.m. Closed on Sundays.

B&B INSIDE A PALACE

In the city centre, besides the big historical and all recently restored hotels like Villa Igiea Hilton, Hotel delle Palme, Excelsior, Grand Hotel Wagner, Grand Hotel Piazza Borsa, Centrale Palace, you can also stay in a comfortable B&B inside the restored aristocratic buildings. You cannot miss some of them for the charm that recalls the deeds of The Leopard novel. It is advisable to stay in the rooms of the Mezzanino del Gattopardo situated in via Alloro. Another four stars B&B is the Quattro Quarti in a building that stands on corso Vittorio Emanuele in a quiet alley of Giardino dell'Alloro. Another atmosphere that recalls The Leopard novel can be found in a building called Ajutamicristo in corso Garibaldi and in the nearest Dimora del Genio or Palazzo Speciale in the central piazza Bologni.

Mezzanino del Gattopardo
Address: via Alloro, 145
Tel. 3334771703

Quattro Quarti
Address: corso Vittorio, 376
Tel. 3473367152 - 091583687

Palazzo Ajutamicristo
Address: via Garibaldi, 24
Tel. 0916166342

La Dimora del Genio
Address: via Garibaldi, 58
Tel. 3476587664 - 0916166981

Il Giardino dell'Alloro
Address: vicolo dell'Alloro, 8
Tel. 3382243541

Palazzo Speciale
Address: via M. Puglia, 2
Tel. 3392280193 - 091332173

Above, the elegance of the Liberty style sitting rooms at Villa Igiea, on the right, the facade of the Sanctuary of S. Rosalia on the top of Mount Pellegrino

climb the mountain with any means: the common people used to go on a jackass with the typical decorated carts, the nobles on a carriage, the members of the Senate on the sedan chair.

In the marina of Acquasanta, the Grand Hotel Villa Igiea overlooks the biggest and the most well-equipped harbour of the city. Villa Igiea was the old private residence of the Florio family, brilliant entrepreneurs of the beginning of the century. Today it is a big hotel and a benchmark for noblemen and the European elite. In the interior there are precious rooms with Liberty style frescos and furniture signed by the architect Ernesto Basile. The Tonnara Florio stands at the fishing harbour of Arenella. Today it

is a private residence, restaurant and pub on the beach. Another Tonnara used for open-air dinners and music is the Tonnara Bordonaro of Vergine Maria, in the summer you can have dinner and listen to jazz music next to the beach among the fishermen's houses.

Once you get to Mondello, among the sea clubs on the beach and the Liberty style villas, you can go towards the Charleston bathing establishment where you can rent a deckchair, a canoe or a windsurf even for few hours. The establishment, built at the beginning of the century, includes a restaurant having the same name, with its terraces on the light blue water from where you can admire the entire bay framed by Mount Pellegrino and Capo Gallo that in the last few years have become a protected area. From the square of Mondello, among bars and small tables you can walk towards the entrance of the natural reserve of Mount Gallo. ■

NEW MUSEUMS YOU CANNOT MISS

Modern Art Gallery

The impressive architectonical complex of Sant'Anna alla Misericordia hosts 216 selected works of art, 178 paintings, 38 sculptures that outline the new aspect of the Modern Art Gallery inaugurated in 2006. It is situated between the recovered spaces of the monumental building of the former school and the 17th-century aristocratic building.

It contains the masterpieces of Mario Sironi, Fausto Pirandello, Felice Casorati, Massimo Campigli, Pietro Consagra, Emilio Greco, Renato Guttuso and other Sicilian and foreign artists with literally rediscovered important works of art.

Address: via S.Anna 21

Tel. 0918431605

Opening: Tue and Sun 9.30 a.m.18.30 p.m.

International Museum of the Puppets

It stands in the new seat of piazzetta Niscemi and includes 3500 pieces of Sicilian puppets, Neapolitan glove puppets and marionettes from all over the world.

Very notable is the department dedicated to the Eastern models. Three of the departments are dedicated to the Opera of the Puppets, the traditional theatre of the Southern Italy inspired by the knightly epic in the several schools of Palermo, Catania and Naples.

Address: piazzetta Niscemi, 5

Tel. 091328060

Opening: 9 a.m. to 1 p.m. - 3.30 to 6.30 p.m.

From Mon to Fry

Closed on holydays

Fields and vineyards, in the background the snows of Etna, the highest volcano in Europe

02 IN-AND-AROUND THE PARKS
THE NEBRODI, THE ETNA AND THE MADONIE

The natural parks are the most surprising areas of Sicily. The Madonie and the Nebrodi have snowy mountaintops, forest trees and protected flora and fauna that prove the meeting between the Mediterranean and the Northern-Europe habitats. The big volcano called Etna surrounded by the park and the piedmont little countries

The Nebrodi

The Sicily of the mountains and woods standing on the Tyrrhenian coast, from the sea to the high altitude woods is a real heaven to discover step-by-step and season-by-season.
On the Nebrodi you can find small villages with hidden masterpieces and very ancient cultures linked to the work of the land and the cattle breeding, they are populated by shepherds, charcoal burners, horse-breeders, ceramic and loom craftsmen.
Along the freeway A 20, once you get past the Tindari promontory that falls off a cliff on a sand lagoon formed by undercurrent jets, you can reach the park from several directions: from Sant'Agata di Militello, Acquedolci, Cesarò or Caronia. Few kilometres from Acquedolci, there is an old villa that today is a charming holyday farm called Villa Nicetta, you can spend the night there and the day in the countryside in order to taste a very good typical cheese dish. It is advisable especially for those who travel with children; it is owner-occupied and run. It offers a very good cooking: freshly made macaroni covered with sprouts or pork meat sauce, second dishes made of vegetables and roasted food and, at the end, the "pignoccata al miele" (local dessert made of fried pastry-balls covered with honey).

THE NEBRODI'S PARK

Founded in 1993, it includes 23 districts in the protected area and preserves the biggest wooded formation of Sicily (50.000 hectares) and 17 visitor's centres scattered on the territory.
Coast centres:
Santo Stefano di Camastra
Address: via Umberto
Tel. 0921331199
S. Agata Militello
Address: via Cosenza, 149
Tel. 0941705934
Website: www.parcodeinebrodi.it
The folklore you cannot miss:
"Festa del Muzzuni" in Alcara li Fusi, 24th June;
"Madonna della Luce" in Mistretta, 8th September

On the left, a promenade to go along in a mountain bike. Above, Alcara Li Fusi, one of the gems of the Nebrodi's park. In the background the Rock of Crasto where the griffons are flying again

Leaving behind the sea of Sant'Agata, along the provincial street 161 you can get to a village called Alcara li Fusi where the park has opened a small visitor centre that shows the environment of raptorial like the eagle and the griffon both circling on the calcareous tops of the Nebrodi. On the left, in the district Grazia, over the sport camp, you cannot miss a walk around the Rocche del Crasto, a complex of rose rocks of the Dolomites where you can go see the griffon circling; there is a colony of 40 big raptorial animals that is now perfectly naturalized and nested there. The wingspan of the griffons reaches 3 metres; you can see them at close range together with the licensed guides that arrange walks and bird watching by booking (Tel. 3472927684, 3475794695 from 9 a.m. to 5 p.m.).

Leaving Alcara, the street brings towards Portella Gazzara and reaches 1000 metres of altitude. On your right you can see the big forests of Mangaliviti, the woods of Miraglia and Solazzo Verde. You can find from the oak groves to beeches and the sessile oaks. In Portella, in the visitor centre of the park (Tel. 3475335079), it is possible to rent a bike

SPEND THE NIGHT BY THE NEBRODI

Villa Nicetta

Small and well furnished apartments situated in front of the eighteen-century manor. It also includes a chapel.
Wide garden, porch with an external area used for open-air meals, vegetables and local production of cheese.
Open all year round
Address: district Nicetta, 98070, Acquedolci (ME)
Tel. and Fax: 0941726142
Rates: 75 euros half board

Villa Miraglia

Mountain style, in the middle of a park, few kilometres away from the lake Biviere, with Sicilian traditional furnishing, it only has 5 plain rooms and a rustic kitchen. Plunged among the woods, during summer you can make a ride by bike or horse with a guide.
Address: highway 289 Cesarò (ME)
Tel. and Fax: 095697397
Rates: 70 euros half board, 40 euros B&B

Atelier sul Mare

Hotel and museum, you can stay in 15 art rooms or in standard doubles or triples with sea view, equipped beaches and pottery. Tour guide on request to the Fiumara d'Arte.
Closed in November
Address: Castel di Tusa, via Cesare Battisti, 4 Messina (ME)
Tel. 0921334295
Rates: 140 euros the double art room, 100 euros the standard.

The forest trees, in the background the eruption of the Mount Etna. Below, on the right, the beech wood of Mount Soro, a real heaven for trekkers

THE ETNA'S PARK

Ente Parco Etna
Address: via Convento, 45 95030, Nicolosi
Tel. 095821111, tourist bureau, 095821205

Centro di Educazione Ambientale
Address: via Abate Meli, 17
Tel. 095955159

Visiting centre:
Linguaglossa
Address: piazza Annunziata, 5
Tel. 095643094

Randazzo
Address: piazza Municipio
Tel. 0957991611
Website: www.parcoetna.it

Private guide service:
Geo Etna
Tel. 3496109957
Rates: Jeep and guide 75 euros

for a mountain tour or drive down the valley of the stream Rosmarino towards the small village Longi where it is worth to make a stopover to see the stone mill belonging to the miller Umberto Russo in via Santa Croce. Here, you can try the old home-baked biscuits with almonds and pistachios, and the wholemeal bread (Tel. 3493424964). By following the road signs on the provincial street 157 towards Rocca di Caprileone you will meet, after about 10 kilometres on the right, a villa with a huge terrace overlooking the panoramic view of the see and the Aeolian Islands: it is the old restaurant Antica Filanda, (Tel. 0941919704) also mentioned by the Gambero Rosso[*1] and the guidebook Osterie d'Italia. It is a must-see for sophisticated gourmets. On a covered terrace or in a small wine shop made of stones, you can try a very refined Sicilian cooking: ravioli, au-

*1 Italian food and wine magazine.

THE MOUNT **ETNA**

You can get there from Messina, driving along the motorway ME-CT, go towards the A 18 until the Giarre exit sign in the direction of Zafferana. Those who come from Palermo can take the motorway PA-CT A 19 until the ring road towards Messina, and then take the A 18 ME-CT until the Giarre exit sign towards Zafferana down to the street of the volcano.

The Mount Etna is relatively young; the first eruptions go back to five hundred thousand years ago and we count at least 135 of them. The most tragic and famous was the one that in 1669 partially destroyed Catania and reached the sea lasting 122 days non-stop. On its slopes there are citrus and fruit orchards, luxuriant terraced vineyards (where the full-bodied wine of the Etna is produced) and olive trees that produce good quality oil. Over 500 metres of altitude the excellent growing of almond, hazel and pistachio trees starts. A little bit higher there are the oaks, the majestic chestnut woods, the wide spot of the pines, beeches and birches standing among strong and wild scented Spanish broom paths. At the end, over 2000 metres of altitude, there are wide lava fields covered with moss, lichen, small thorny bushes of Christ's-thorn, wreaths of soapwort and Anthemis, sprigs of Aetnensis violets, and other endemic species of flowers, last trace of the vegetable life. There are two places you should know: Nicolosi and Linguarossa. In both places you can find skiing facilities and centres where you can rent skis, ski boots, ski pole and other outfits. In autumn, in both places, wide and superior is the picking of mushrooms also prepared in cooperation with the local expert organizations. You can serve them at table in many delicious versions or celebrate in great mushroom-festivals on Sundays in October and November. But the real discovery of the volcano can be done with the trekking or with the tour guides; from the small walks, to the three-days crossing and the camp. All you have to do is choose on the park website or pick one of the many qualified societies. At last, we have three suggestions to make an unusual visit to the volcano: with the Circumetnea, an old steam train of the beginning of the century to get to the station of Catania Borgo, it goes along the original path with stopovers in the historic sites; with the cable cars of the Etna cableway that from the Rifugio Sapienza will bring you to 2504 of altitude in 15 minutes, from there you can keep walking or drive a jeep until 3000 metres of altitude; with the Air Panarea tour flight. It takes off from Catania, flies over the Mount Etna and heads for the Aeolian Islands to admire the Vulcano and Stromboli Islands. It is as much as to say: three volcanoes with one trip.

bergines and ricotta cheese rolls, pesto from Bronte, pork with chestnuts, prickly pears and grape aspics.

Before you go to San Marco d'Alunzio, the city of crafts, looms and gastronomic specialties, make a detour via the small centre of Mirto in order to visit the Fashion Museum inside the Palazzo Cupane. It shows beautiful clothes, bottom drawers and accessories that recall the period of the Leopard novel until the twentieth century Liberty style, given by noblewomen of the big islander families (via Cupani, Tel. 0941919068). Back to the highway 113, few kilometres later, there is a crossroads for Caronia. You can reach it after 4 kilometres of panoramic streets full of bends. Once you get past the settled area dominated by a private castle, you can walk up on the left among the wonderful oak wood, then, leaving behind the sea and the Aeolian Islands you can reach Portella dell'Obolo after 22 kilometres. From here, the path bringing to the walking tour around the Tassita wood and the teaching area of the coal start. The wood is a very old-formed botanical relict; it stretches for 50 hectares and shows sizeable specimens of yew trees (Taxus Baccata) with trunks entirely covered with moss. Towards the district Moglia, following the path on the left you get to a big stone fountain with drinkable water. If you go on for less than one kilometre you will find an enclosed wooden area with yew trees and a small wooden stairs entrance. Very remarkable is the coalfield, four areas for the gathering of the wood, the placing of the fussuni*2 in a circle, the preparation of the woodpile, later covered with earth and leaves until the burning phase.

In springtime you can go walking or riding in the Biviere di Cesarò, going along the lake Maulazzo, an artificial basin surrounded by a wonderful cork forest that in winter is covered by a heavy blanket of snow. Here we are at almost 1300 metres in the domain of the holm oak and the maple

Horse trips along the alleys in the park, on the right the beauty of the landscape of Biviere di Cesarò

*2 Rounded placing of the woodpile around a core made of dry wood or bad-cooked coal.

The medieval district of Castiglione di Sicilia in the province of Catania, food-and-wine excellent location, below, on the right, some pictures of the 2003 eruption of the Etna Mount

SPEND THE NIGHT BY THE MOUNT ETNA

Villa Lionti
Address: via Lombardo, 54 (CT)
Tel. 0941361681

Az. Scammacca del Murgo
Address: via Zafferana, 13 - S.Venerina (CT)
Tel. 095950520

Villa Paradiso dell'Etna
Address: via per Viagrande, 37 - S. Giovanni La Punta (CT)
Tel. 0957512409

Sotto il Vulcano B&B
Address: via Manpilieri – Nicolosi (CT)
Tel. 095914851

Borgo Petra B&B
Address: via Teatro 9 – Mascalucia (CT)
Tel. 0957277184

with the magnificent specimen in the Mount Soro area that reaches 22 metres of height.
By car, you can get to Portella Femmina Morta by following the provincial road 168; there, you can leave your car; 2 kilometres more and, after the asphalt road on your left, the dirt patch that briskly brings to lake Malauzzo starts. 4 more difficult kilometres and you can get to the artificial basin of Biviere. If you want to spend the night or make a stopover in a plain shelter you can stop at Villa Miraglia with its 5 rooms and very good homemade dishes. From here, if you want to visit the castle Ducea di Nelson, it is advisable to go back to the road 289 towards Cesarò and go towards Maniace for 15 kilometres, passing through very beautiful woods. The castle, 13 kilometres outside the built-up area, has a small and lovely rose garden in the inside (Tel. 095690018). Since the restoration work of the Santa Maria di Maniace Abbey is over, it is possible to visit the apartment of the dukes with period paintings and fur-

TREKKING ON THE ETNA, MONTE NERO DEGLI ZAPPINI

There is nothing more relaxing than walking under the volcano during the clear and still mild Sicilian autumn, among the luxury nature of the Etna, orchards, prickly pears and forest trees. From Nicolosi, where in an old monastery the park of the Etna has its seat, you can drive a jeep towards the south side of the crater.

"A muntagna", that is the way local people call it, is more than ever changeable and unpredictable: wind, fog, even ash rain are not unusual in this mountain roads because of the volcanic activity. Leaving behind the Monti Rossi, small craters covered with thick wood, you can start walking from the entrance of the Monte Nero degli Zappini path in the district of Serra La Nave, the oldest and most popular path for the walkers of the area. The name definitely comes from a toponymic mistake; it should have been Neve (snow). We are at about 1000 metres of altitude on the southwest side of the volcano. Once you park your jeep near the astrophysical observatory, take a path that winds up for about two hours along an easy up and down of sand among Spanish brooms, pines, chestnut trees where the old and the recent lava, with its colours and shapes, is the main attraction. After about one kilometre, make a stopover to the botanical garden Nuova Gussonea. Once you get past the pines forest trees, on your right you can see the central crater with its degassing plume of smoke, and the small one, both recognizable by the brown and yellow shades. The volcano imposes a continuous evolution of what surrounds it, it is the boss of everything, it defines the landscape, the vegetation, it covers houses and orchards, it generates streams of rocks, hills, caves and craters. Complete your walk at the Galvarina meeting-place at 1900 metres of altitude. It has a terrace with a panoramic view on the active crater and a fountain. If you are ready to go back, put your face up in order to sight the rare eagle that lives in tandem on these inaccessible rocks.

In the small built-up area of San Pietro in Clarenza you can spend the night at Villa Lionti, charming residence that during the nineteenth century was a wine farm as shown by the mill to press grapes at the entrance. There, you will be plunged into the perfume of the jasmine, datura, lavender and the good old laces. Not far from there is the farm holiday San Michele belonging to the baron Scammacca del Murgo, renowned for the red wines of the Etna.

niture. The building dates back to the 1147 Norman period. Worth mentioning is the entrance of the abbey, with its wonderful pointed vault portal with particular anthropomorphic sculptures. The English admiral Horatio Nelson received the monumental complex as a gift by Ferdinand II after the victory of Trafalgar, but he never lived there.

It is advisable to stop in Cesarò in order to have lunch in the restaurant Mazzurco (Tel. 0957732100), a modern and tidy place that serves amazing delicacies with local pistachios, pistachio-filled ravioli, cream puff and cannolo (Sicilian pastry roll) filled with pistachio and fillet covered with pistachio sauce. A tasty stopover can be made in the nearest district of San Fratello in order to taste local desserts with almonds and pistachios called with dialect names.

The Madonie

You can get to the park from the coast road 113 following the road signs towards Castelbuono, the Ventimiglia village that stands around the mighty castle. The centre of Castelbuono, 9 kilometres away, was founded in 1269 by Alduino Ventimiglia, count of Geraci and lord of the Madonie. Starting from the square near the castle, you can visit the interior of

A detail of the balcony of the Mother Church of Petralia Soprana, on the right a view of the old town centre of Castelbuono at dawn, in the background the profile of the Madonie

THE MADONIE'S PARK

The park gathers 15 districts and has an entire reserved area of 5.377 hectares.

Geopark Museums – two museums of the geologic history of the park in Petralia Sottana and Caltavuturo.

Le vie dell'Arte – seven works of contemporary art located in the most interesting places.

Address: Petralia Sottana - via P. Agliata, 16

Tel. 0921684011

Website: www.parcodellemadonie.it

the manor house built in 1316 by Francesco Ventimiglia in order to defend the city. It has a small palatine chapel dedicated to Saint Anne, baroque treasure with the stuccoworks by Serpotta's brothers made at the end of the seventeenth century. The castle hosts the Civic Museum with sacred and contemporary works of art. Walking down the main street you can get to piazza Margherita with its sixteenth-century fountain in the middle and the Madrice Vecchia di Maria Assunta (14th century) on the left with its beautiful Gothic-Catalan porch. A must-see is the small museum Minà Palumbo that keeps the valuable nineteenth-century herbarium as a scientific documentation of the flora and the fauna of the Madonie. Today, in the A zone of the park, over 1600 botanical species and at least 80 rare butterflies survive. In the main square there is a tasting of desserts

CHARMING AND GASTRONOMIC **FARM HOLIDAYS**

In San Giovanni, farm district of a hundred people, lost in the green domain of the wheat in the Madonie, you can go take shelter among the silence of the fields and the wood around the district of Petralia Soprana.

The Masseria San Giovanni Sgadari (Tel. 0921687243 – Rates: 90 euros double room and B&B suite from 150 to 200 euros) is one of the newest inside the park. The beautiful structure is almost hidden by the crossroads of Madonnuzza, in the district of Fasanò, 8 km from Petralia Sottana.

The Madonie is also a box of ancient and unforgettable flavours: the goat's milk ricotta cheese, even tastier during the spring because of the plenty pasturages, useful to season the home-made pasta together with other ingredients, vegetable appetizers, pork meat, salami and sausages, cheese desserts, the oldest is the "sfoglio" from Polizzi Generosa, delicious mixture made of tuma cheese, chocolate and cinnamon wrapped up by a short pastry. In order to make a full immersion in the gastronomy of the Madonie, take a weekend cooking class and taste old dishes with new combination of flavours, you can stop in Donalegge, after the village of Castellana, small land known for its desserts, biscuits and chocolate. Here, on the hills of the right side of the highway 120, you can find the holiday farm **Donalegge al Castellazzo**, with the elegant restaurant "La Forchetta del Barone". You cannot miss some reinvented dishes such as the vegetable strudel with cheese, the vegetable couscous, the roast seasoned with fennel sauce, the plum jam tart. Charming places, delicate coloured walls, a modern fireplace in each room and quick stone exteriors.

The two-floor farm has 11 rooms with sober and elegant furniture. During the summer, in order to relieve the Sicilian heat, there is the open-air swimming pool placed on the fields and the garden from where you can pick up and buy broad beans, lentils and tomatoes. You can also buy delicious first-pressing extra-virgin olive oil.

Tel. 092687190

Rates: 65 euros B&B, 90 euros half board.

Driving towards Tre Monzelli you can see on your left a small farm street that brings you to the valley for 3 km and leads to the farm **Feudo San Giorgio**. The owners made it a real heaven for those who travel with children. There are paddocks, a swimming pool and a big adventure playground. The comfortable and large apartments are placed around the courtyard; the farm stands among the hills like a fortress. The country-style restaurant, situated in the big pallet and the cart shelters, offers a simple and very tasty cooking made of homemade pasta, pappardelle with wild vegetables and fresh ricotta cheese, vegetable omelettes, grilled meat and biological beef.

Tel. 0921642613,

Rates: 45 euros per person B&B, 65 euros half board

02

of Fiasconaro, you cannot miss the delicious Sicilian "mannetto" (spiced brioche with sultanas) filled with delicious food and orange peel. 20 kilometres from Castelbuono following the highway 286 you will find Geraci Siculo that climbs among torrents and woods until 1000 metres of altitude. Geraci, at the foot of the mountain Catarineci seems to be protected by the ridges. This Arab village extended with the Ventimiglia family around 1200; at that time the district became a real city-state before the court moved to Castelbuono.
In August, there is the Giostra dei Ventimiglia, commemoration in period costumes that livens up the old city. In order to go down towards the sea of Cefalù, that is included in the park area, you can choose to take back the same road, or go along the inner itinerary that passes through the oak wood of Gibilmanna and the Sanctuary. From far away you can see the lovely country villages of Isnello and Gratteri, a peaceful oasis for your vacation. From

A detail of the balcony of the Mother Church of Petralia Soprana, on the right a view of the old town centre of Castelbuono at dawn, in the background the profile of the Madonie

SPEND THE NIGHT BY THE MADONIE

Relais Santa Anastasia
It is a medieval district with a wine cellar.
Address: district Santa Anastasia - 90013 Castelbuono (PA)
Tel. and Fax: 0921672233 **Rates:** double standard 210 euros in B&B

Vecchio Frantoio
Big farm made of stones, plunged among olive groves, it offers oil production.
Address: district Firrione-Scillato (PA)
Tel. 0921663047
Rates: 50 euros per person in B&B, restaurant 25 euros

Masseria Susafa
Plunged in the Sicily of the wheat, there are 13 rooms inside the manor.
Address: district Susafa, Polizzi Generosa (PA)
Tel. 3389608713
Rates: B&B 45 euros, half board 60 euros

Gli Alberi del Paradiso
50 rooms inside the wide building plunged in the green fields, 1 km from the equipped beach.
Address: via dei Mulini 18, Cefalù (PA)
Tel. 0921423900
Rates: double room B&B from 98 to 260 euros

Belli Resort
It has 11 rooms, 3 suites inside a typical 19th-century farmhouse, a swimming pool and a spa.
Address: via Roma 58, Gratteri (PA)
Tel. 091905666
Rates: from 70 to 90 euros

The old harbour of Cefalù, on the right the vineyards of the farm Sant'Anastasia near Castelbuono

the crossroads towards the Sanctuary along the provincial road 54, after 15 kilometres of winding road you will get to the coast of Cefalù. The Norman city of Roger II lies down around the big rock from where you can make out the ruins of the Diana temple, very old place of worship, and the Byzantine strengthen castle. The city was captured by the Arabs in 858 and finally taken back by the count Roger II of Sicily in 1130 when the building of the Cathedral started. The oldest core of the district is Giudecca with the megalithic walls recovered in a cliff falling sheer to the beach. The old medieval town expanded over both sides of corso Ruggero, enriched today by small shops, restaurants and meeting places.

From the street on the right you can go to the promenade; it takes at least one hour walking briskly. Still on corso Ruggero there is the facade of the Osterio Magno (XIII) used today as an exhibition area. Once you get past the old harbour you can see the medieval wash-house. Before you leave the city centre visit the building of the baron Mandralisca with the museum that gathers art and archaeology collections of the wonderful Sicilian-made furniture of the eighteenth-century. In summer, the museum hosts live concerts in the terrace. Besides the equipped beach on the sea front, Cefalù offers several sea places among rocks and narrow gorges; one of the most popular is Kalura, sheltered by the tourist har-

RELAIS SANT'ANASTASIA IN CASTELBUONO, A HOLIDAY IN A WINE CELLAR

Green hills covered with vineyards, and the Mediterranean scrub that in springtime gives off colours and delightful perfumes, it stands on the sea of Sant'Ambrogio and on the sandy and rocky coast of Finale di Pollina; on the background you can see the Madonie mountains. Here we are, along the highway that from Palermo brings to Messina. On the back there is the Rock of Cefalù with its square outline leaning forward over the Tyrrhenian Sea. After six kilometres towards Castelbuono you can get to the entrance of the relay Sant'Anastasia. Here, around a small countryside abbey that dates back to the XI century, maybe the oldest of the area, there is a functional and elegant resort with 25 rooms and 3 suites, all with a view on the vineyards. Very beautiful is the quick stone building, undamaged despite the changing from private residence to excellent accommodation facility. It has a big yard with a small church still used for the Sunday and holiday Mass. The rooms are called with the names of the local wines. For example: Ciliegiolo (cherry liqueur), where the predominant colour is red and Cabernet with white sheds. They all have a sea view; they are large and particularly furnished with the greatest care. Corte dell'Abate has two dining rooms and only the guests of the relay can have breakfast with a view on the swimming pool. Apart from the 450 hectares all vineyards in a really enviable position, what really shines in Sant'Anastasia is the very fine wines that they produce that in the last few years are named in the top ten. There are 12 labels in all. The red wines Nerello Mascalese, Nero d'Avola, Passomaggio, made from Nero d'Avola and Merlot local vines, Montenero and Litra, cabernet sauvignon, are the most renowned and difficult to find in wine shops in the last few years.
The wine bar is open also in February, only moment of break for the relay that opens again in March. It is possible to deliver wine abroad.

bour. Out of the city, in the road 113 towards Buonfornello and Palermo, there are the big beaches of Settefrati and Mazzaforno; they stand near holyday clubs and residences hidden by olive groves.

The backcountry of the Madonie

Scillato and Polizzi are the first two small villages of the inner side of the Madonie; they are big natural lungs with good accommodation facilities. The open road, where the endurance automobile race Targa Florio was held, goes up winding among very old olive trees and the districts of Firrione towards Collesano and Polizzi Generosa. After a couple of kilometres you will see the old oil mill where you can buy some olive oil and spend the night in comfortable recently-restored double or quadruple rooms and taste the plain cooking of the Madonie. Sweep the mountain amphitheatre of the Quacelle, wonderful complex of dolomitic rocks on the left and the entire reserve of the park in the A zone. On the crossroads for Polizzi, you can skirt the built-up area. From here, the panoramic view opens up on the right on the Imera valley that stretches as far as the eye can see on the inner part of the Sicily full of fields of wheat. The name Generosa (generous) was assigned by Fredrick II; it was a culture and art centre, shelter destination for nobles and sovereigns such as Elizabeth of Aragon and Blanche of Navarre. There are several churches and noble residences worth to visit. A worthy stopover is the MAM Madonita Museum in Palazzo Notarbartolo that contains missing specimens of the fauna. Next to the museum you will see the entrance of a garden

Woods and landscapes of the high Madonie. On the right the Church Commenda in Polizzi Generosa. Below a view of the Golf Club "Le Madonie"

that contains a small private lodge with a lookout on a wide hazel grove valley, the speciality of the area. You cannot miss the tasting of the "sfoglio" the local dessert made of ricotta cheese, the seasoned pumpkin, chocolate and cinnamon. Going out of the village, under the arches, you can take the provincial road 119 that brings to the crossroads of Portella Colla and Piano Battaglia. Before you get to the amphitheatre of the Quacelle and the Portella, on the right there is a gate, State Forestry Department property that marks the boundary of an unsurfaced road that brings to Vallona Madonna degli Angeli. Leave there your car and take the unsurfaced road that from an altitude of 1400 metres goes to 1600, with two hours walking uphill you can get to the valley. In the middle of a rocky ridge, the last 30 specimens of Abies nebrodensis live isola-

ted. They are a real botanical rarity, relict of the last glaciation. Once you go back to the highway 120, drive towards Castellana and Petralie.

Petralia Sottana, of very ancient, maybe Roman, origins can be distinguished by the name from the higher Soprana. There are beautiful 15th and 6th century churches like the Mother Church with its Latin Cross that stands on a breathtaking lookout on Mount San Salvatore. Soprana, stands on a site that dates back to the period of the Sicani, situated at 1147 metres of altitude, it was very successful as a barn during the Roman period. In 1602, it was captured by the count Roger of Altavilla that built the main churches, such as Santa Maria in Loreto, sheltered by the old Norman fortress in the district "castru" and the Church of Madre di San Pietro e Paolo (9th century). Drive back towards Palermo and get to Campofelice di Roccella, make a detour via the 18 holes-golf course "Le Madonie". The particularly beautiful green space, surrounded by olive and citrus trees stretches on the mountains and the sea of the gulf of Termini. ■

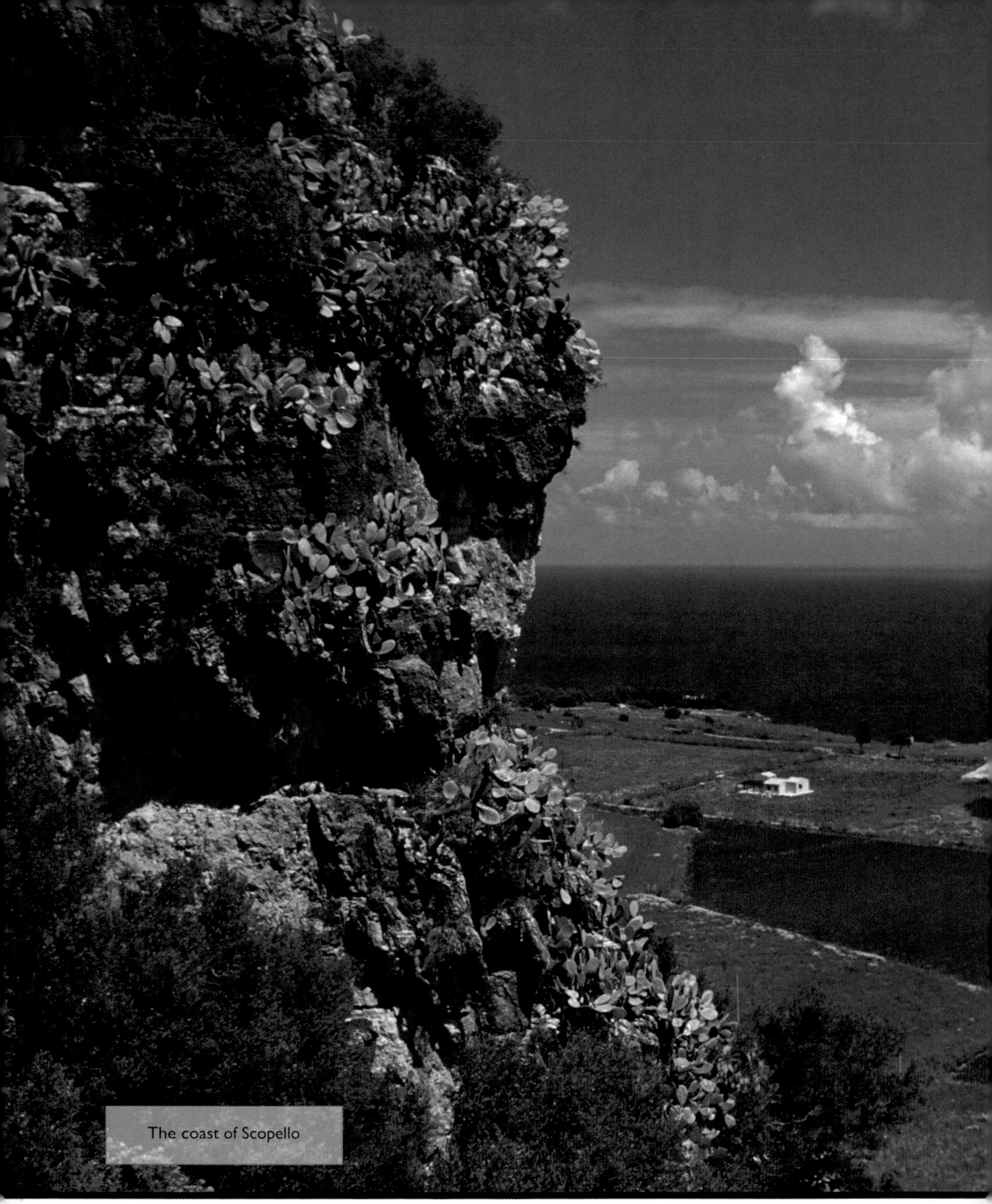

The coast of Scopello

03

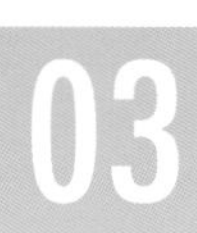

THE COUNTRY RESORTS
THROUGH SEA AND VINEYARDS

Rediscovered thanks to the America's Cup, Trapani's districts are a heaven of sea, wind, coasts and countrysides. Take a look at the natural reserve of the Zingaro and the landscape of the Saline, the Mount Erice and the surrounding country scattered with old yards that turned into holiday farms and resorts

Full of small fortresses of stone with a wide yard in the middle, heavens of peace plunged in vineyards and olive groves stretching as far as the eye can see, usually down to the seaside. The African sea of the western Sicily with its blinding light shining on the outline of the Aegadian Islands, laying there, as at the hands of a producer, in front of the coast.

In Sicily, there are several yards to suit all tastes and each one has a different story. Some yards have turned into hotels with a bar service near the swimming pool and some other have become small resorts with a fireplace inside the room and sophisticated towels with noble coat of arms. Even though they are holiday farms in flourishing and full activity, they are still modernized farms where every day, the old traditions of the Sicilian country are shared: the bread hot from the oven "cunzato" (filled) with olive oil, anchovies and rosemary served into a room pervaded by the good smell of wine and barrels.

From the Arabic "bahahss" that means fortified yard with a tower and city walls, in some cases they have turned into medieval castles by the Normans arrived in Sicily with Roger I. There are also farmlands, used for defensive purposes that once used to give hospitality to farm workers, animals, production and manufacturing process of the wine and olive oil.

EVENTS YOU CANNOT MISS
GO TO SAN VITO FOR THE COUSCOUS FEST

The guru of the kitchen Edoardo Raspelli nominated it the dish of the peace among the people. At the end of September in San Vito Lo Capo the Couscous Fest is celebrated. Besides the competition between international chefs, along the main street of the small fisherman's town near Trapani the Slow Food Association prepares laboratories of taste for the local productions: wine, olive oil, almond desserts, cheese and preserves. In the square, the ethnic music concerts and the exhibition stands liven up the night of San Vito recreating a perfect Mediterranean atmosphere. As a matter of fact, in San Vito and in the entire Trapani coast, from Mazara del Vallo to Marsala down to the Aegadian Islands the couscous goes well with the fabulous fish soup called "ghiotta" (tasty). How and when it arrived from Maghreb, where is strictly cooked with meat is really hard to say as well as following all the changes linked to the type of fish, vegetables and spice used. Into the sophisticated tasty broth the ingredients that cannot miss are: grouper, scorpion fish, teleost fish, conger eel and cuttlefish. Marilù Terrasi in her Pocho (Tel. 0923972525), small guesthouse furnished with ethnic taste that overlooks the Makari bay few kilometres away from San Vito, organizes gastronomic laboratories on Sundays. If you want to spend the night on the beach of San Vito you can go to the sophisticated hotel also wellness centre Capo San Vito (Tel. 0923972122).

The countrysides near Trapani, have been involved for centuries in the production of white and dessert wines, popular all over the world. They hold a record in one of the most generous regions for the production of grapes all over Italy. Here are the main streets of the Sicilian wine, the itinerary that brings to the revival of the authentic Marsala wine, recently recognized as DOC (Controlled origin denomination) in order to keep it safe from the imitations. There is the street of Bianco d'Alcamo, the street of the Inzolia and Menfi at the boundary with Agrigento or the street of the Passito that leads to Pantelleria.

Here, people have recently intensified the cultivation of local extra-virgin olive trees such as the "Biancolilla" and the big oval "Nocellara del Belice" from where you can take a fine, strong and scented olive oil with no trace of acidity.

In the top on the left, the waters of the Stagnone in a canoe, next to it the preparation of the couscous of San Vito Lo Capo, below on the left the entrance of Baglio Fontana in Buseto Palizzolo

The first Trapani yard that revived in the spirit of the high quality tourism is Baglio Santacroce, a beautiful quick stone structure; it almost looks like a small monastery between the sea and the countryside. You can get there by following the motorway to-

FROM THE **TONNARA OF SCOPELLO** TO THE **TEMPLE OF SEGESTA**

Few kilometres from the Zingaro, the first Sicilian natural reserve, overlooking the delightful gulf of Castellammare, you can get to Scopello, the town made of stones cast on the Tonnara and its stacks.

The Tonnara, operative until few past decades ago, has a yard with a small church and a way down that brings straight to the beach and offers the chance to spend a week in two elegant apartments with wonderful terraces with a view on the gulf but without TV, phone and air conditioner (Tel. 3386419133). This marvellous location, also well described by the TV series of the Commissario Montalbano, is so charming because of the waves and the deep blue of the explorable waters. From the Tonnara towards the provincial road 187 that brings to the town of Castellammare del Golfo, old harbour of Segesta, there is a series of creeks, little coves such as Guidaloca that has two small restaurants called Calarossa and Calabianca easily accessible walking through carob paths, olive trees and dwarf palms. Once you get past the town, the road signs will bring you to the archaeological park of Segesta, seat of summer shows in the suggestive old theatre. After 7 km, take a sulphurous bath in the Segesta baths or down in the hot river that through a green canyon laps against natural hot and protective springs.

The road goes on through a valley full of vineyards and beds of reeds up to the top of a hill where there is the big Dorian temple, built by the Elymians on the foundation of the big city of Segesta, and able to defeat even Selinunte. If you want to visit the archaeological park and arrive up to the theatre, you can take a shuttle or follow a path from where you can admire the remains of the towers, the walls and the squares.

wards Trapani, getting past the built-up area of Valderice and the district under the Mount Erice. Saved by the decay of the 70s, the yard was entirely rebuilt in order to turn it into a comfortable hotel; the rooms are around the austere court while the dining rooms have been built all over again in an added structure. Very good is the cooking with fish dishes; as a matter of fact, the restaurant is usually crowded for holiday and Sunday meals. More quite are the small terrace and the Mediterranean garden standing on the blue bay of Mount Cofano, plunged in an almost surrealistic silence between fields and sea. The rooms, some of them still have the typical 18th-century suspended platforms and the grating on the windows, are furnished with period Sicilian fittings such as wrought iron headboards, sacristy chairs and wonderful coloured carpets coming from the last working looms of the shops of the near medieval town Erice, few kilometres away.

Along the panoramic street that brings to Castellammare, out of the nice little town Buseto Palizzolo, great starting point for trips towards the well-known white beach of San Vito Lo Capo, another well-preserved yard is Baglio Fontana situated in the middle of hundreds of hectares of cultivated vineyards. The family-owners have recently restored the entire noble floor for the guests and opened a swimming pool with a hydromassage in the private garden. In this yard a great Nero d'Avola wine is produced together with several types of flavoured-honey that the chef suggests combined

The temple of Segesta, in the top on the right the yard Duca di Castelmonte at the gates of Trapani

SPEND THE NIGHT IN THE YARDS

Baglio Fontanasalsa
Address: via Cusenza, 78 - Fontanasalsa (TP)
Tel. 0923591001
Rates: high season, double room 100 euros
Full board 110 euros per person

Duca di Castelmonte
Address: via Salvatore Motisi, 3 - district Xitta (TP)
Tel. 0923526139
Rates: high season B&B 42 euros per person,
half board 60 euros

with local cheese such as caciocavallo (gourd-shaped cheese), pecorino (sheep's milk cheese) and primosale (mature cheese). From here, you can make a trip to the archaeological area of Segesta, perhaps at sunset when the tuffaceous stones of the Dorian temple turn yellow-orange. Driving back towards Trapani, beyond the big roundabout at 5 kilometres away from the built-up area, you can go on your left towards Paceco and follow the road signs that bring to the old countryside yards. The one belonging to the family Curatolo, named Duca di Castelmonte, still makes an original Sicilian cooking, considering that almost everything (bread, fruit, vegetables, preserves, olive oil and even eggs) is produced in private farms. The homemade recipes have been used for three generations; nothing is invented for Sunday meals or theme-dinners. The couscous, for example, is prepared in front of the guests and served with broccoli and sausages, the fried flat bread with pecorino cheese and vegetables, the busiata, homemade pasta seasoned with ricotta cheese and sausages, the almond caponata*1, the fried pastry with cooked wine and honey. Buy the delicious marmalades of citrus fruits, prickly pears, plums and even tomatoes and the olive oil with the seal of the house. At the Duca di Castelmonte the life goes by with no rules: if the weather is good, starting from Easter, people organize trips to Favignana in rubber dinghy with picnics on board, on Saturday night people have dinner outdoor with a huge buffet while the guitars play Sicilian ballades, early in the morning the wood-burning oven is already on to cook pizzas and flat bread seasoned as one likes: with caciocavallo cheese or other ingredients. You

*1 Sicilian aubergine dish made with chopped fried aubergines, celery and capers, seasoned with sweetened vinegar in a sweet and sour sauce.

SPEND THE NIGHT IN THE YARDS

Baglio Oneto, Framon hotel
Address: contrada Baronazzo Amafi 55 - Marsala (TP)
Tel. 0923746222
Rates: double room 100 euros, half board 65 euros

Baglio Santacroce
Address: via del Cipresso, 1 - Trapani highway - Valderice
Tel. 0923891111
Rates: B&B 56 euros; half board 74 euros

Baglio Basile
Address: highway 115 towards Mazara del Vallo - Petrosino (TP)
Tel. 0923741705
Rates: B&B 56 euros per person; half board 72 euros

can have room service breakfast served in a basket filled with home-baked biscuits and biological marmalades.
More choreographic and tidy is the near Baglio Fontanasalsa. The tables for the lunch are carefully set within the yard, warm and sunny in winter, whereas the dinner is often served in the citrus orchards next to the swimming pool in order to enjoy the local fresh air and the intense orange-blossom smell. Fontanasalsa is also renowned for its local cooking enriched by the gourmets' revisiting. Taste the olive oil ice cream, unusual idea of the chef, the jellies or the ice creams and sorbets made with citrus fruit, prickly pear and pomegranate.
Inside the farms, make a stopover to the old oil mill, the modern production facility where the olive oil is served with homemade bread. Buy the Fontanasalsa fine oil, very intense flavour to use with fish and other dishes.
In the less isolated area among the white houses of Paceo there is Baglio Costadimandorla; four independent apartments built at the end of the 19th century and restored with good taste. The owner is a collector of old majolica objects from Trapani and other items linked to the phases of salt production. The Baglio has a veranda that overlooks the medieval rock of Erice and a small and lovely

A relaxing moment in the coves of the Zingaro natural reserve; on the right the fishing net Tonnara of Scopello

Marsala, the city salon of Piazza Duomo, in the background the monumental complex of S. Pietro

SPEND THE NIGHT IN THE YARDS

Baglio Fontana
Address: Valderice highway - Castellammare
Buseto Palizzolo (TP)
Tel. 0923855000
Rates: double room 100 euros, half board 65 euros

Baglio Costa di Mandorla
Address: via Verderame, 37
Paceco (TP)
Tel. 0923409100 / 3381035806
Rates: apartments for 7 people from 36 to 45 euros

pool placed among the olive trees, it offers a B&B service with homemade citrus or green apple marmalades breakfast. Here, the guests live freely, they can use the bicycles at their disposal for long rides down to the beach of Marausa, 4 kilometres from the near via del Sale. Along the saltpan of Nubia until the landing stage, there is the jewel of the Punic-Phoenician archaeology, the Mozia Island discovered by Pip Whitaker and its new inestimable archaeological museum. Here we are in the natural reserve of the Stagnone, with the incredible shapes of mounds of salt resting under tile pyramids that protect them from the restored windmills.
The street of the salt brings to Baglio Anselmi, regional archaeological museum that keeps the Punic ship found in the waters of the Stagnone. We are near Marsala, Lilybeo for the Phoenicians, Marsahallah in Ara-

bic, with its wonderful 18th-century old town centre. Very impressive is the restoration of the former Complex San Pietro, next to the square of the cathedral, the fish market under the historical vault arches and the former monastery of the Carmine, turned today into a modern art gallery with the old stables used as exhibition area.

Before you get to Marsala, city of the wine and the cellars, you will see on the right Baglio Oneto set down the hills. It is the last resort of the Sicilian group Framon, 48 rooms gathered around the 18th-century tower and the panoramic pool with a view on the Aegadian Islands.

Going into that big yard you can notice that the signs of the past are still written on the old well in the courtyard or on the millstone next to the modern reception. The structure has an 18th-century origin; it was widened to make room to the comfortable suites with a terrace on the pool.

Mazara del Vallo has recently taken the name of "Mazara del Satiro", as written on the road signs, as a tribute to the well-known Hellenic sculpture found in the water of the channel of the fisherman from Ma-

MUSEUMS YOU CANNOT MISS

Satiro Museum

The Satiro of Mazara, 96 kilos of bronze and 2 metres of height, structure of the Hellenistic period, was probably part of a parade for Dionysus. After it represented Italy at the Japanese Expo and after a long exhibition at the Louvre Museum is now on view in Mazara in the former monastery of S. Egedio together with other finds coming from the excavations in the waters of Trapani.

Address: piazza Plebiscito - Mazara del Vallo (TP)
Tel. 0923933917
Opening: Open every day from 9 a.m. to 6 p.m.

Trame Mediterranee Museum

Created in 1996 in the Di Stefano houses, seat of the Orestiadi Foundation, it gathers costumes, jewels, art fabric, ceramic and art items of peoples and cultures of the Mediterranean area: Sicily, Egypt, Tunisia, Palestine, Morocco, Spain, Algeria and Albania. The museum/workshop is the achievement of years of researches, meetings, controversies, surveys and seminars promoted by the Orestiadi Foundation, but it is also a cultural place that has an interdisciplinary nature.

Address: Baglio di Stefano - Gibellina (TP)
Tel. 094267844
Opening: 9 a.m. to 1 p.m. and 3 to 6 p.m. also on Sunday
Closed on Monday

THE SALTPANS OF THE STAGNONE OF MARSALA

From the blue sea to the green lagoon and the white salt, from the liquid to the solid, this is the God blessed miracle according to the lines by the poet from Salina. The warm shades of the Stagnone change with the seasons; a wintry light underlines them as well as the African transparency or the white summery blinding clearness. At night, the red of the dusk is reflected on the sea in a fairytale silence. Since the Roman period, there were working saltpans and, maybe also during the glorious period of Mozia, seawater evaporation tanks. The salt was used in the preservation of fish and meat. Only the shape of the windmills breaks the flat landscape of the Stagnone of Marsala, in the district Nubia and green vineyards far as the eye can see surround it.
These are the hills that produce the fabulous sweet wine of Marsala. A must-see is the Ettore and Infersa mill, wonderful example of productive and environmental restoration. Inside of it, there is a small museum and laboratory of the salt, a big relief map that represents the environment of the saltpan, a conference room for the projection of a video shown to tourists and schools, and even a particular exhibition of jewels made of salt, flour and water that look exactly like the real red coral jewels of Trapani. In June, the manual work of the breaking of the salt goes on, with the help of special metal shovels; it is a very slow and difficult operation because the quality of the salt could be damaged as well as the bottom of the shovels. In September, you can already see the typical pure white mounds along the main banks later placed in big pyramids covered with rough tiles. You can buy the salt of the salt pan in the small shop inside the museum. A must-see is also the Museo del Sale in the district Nubia.

zara and showed in the museum that has the same name. Norman-Arab monuments, baroque churches and Tunisian kasba alleys in the core of the old town surround it. Driving towards the highway 115 Marsala-Mazara, in the district of Petrosino, area of vineyards looking at the African coast, you will find Baglio Basile with its Andalusian white magic of the structure and its boulevard of palms. It was recently restored and open; the area of the Baglio is more quiet and discreet compared to the four stars hotel next to it. The rooms in the upper floor of the old structure look at the sea, they are wide and lovely for the beautiful pastel shades, they have big beds in wrought iron and authentic 19th-century furniture. Stunning is the cobbled paving of the yard and the small church.
From here, two exclusive stopovers are: the memorable Florio cellars, in front of the harbour of Marsala (boo-

Above, the statue of the Giovinetto shown at the Whitaker Museum in Mozia.
Here, the Museo del Sale in the district Nubia

MOZIA, THE PHOENICIAN TREASURE

Re-opened after 2 years of restoration, the small but precious Antiquarium of Mozia gathers Phoenician finds that date back to 7th and 6th century BC, discovered by Giuseppe Whitaker in the excavations of Mozia. In the Middle Ages, the island was called San Pantaleo. Recently restored, today is a real jewel with an open-air bar and a shop where you can buy the wine Tasca d'Almerita, obtained from the grapes grown on the island. You can get there with a comfortable ferryboat that leaves every hour until 7 p.m. from the landing stage along the street that surrounds the Stagnone. Giuseppe Whitaker bought Mozia and in 1905 started digging until he dug up the Phoenician city of the first half of the 7th century. The necropolis, the Tophet, the sacrificial area, the cothon business-landing place and the artificial basin of the Mediterranean ships were dug up too. Whitaker, English entrepreneur and very cultural man, loved living in the house on the island, an elegant building belonging to the museum; next to it there was the house of the attendants, the church and other spaces used as storehouse. Another entirely restored small place is the holiday residence inherited by his daughter Delia and inhabited until the first years of the twentieth century. It was totally restored in the furnishings and the liberty-style fabrics rescuing also the flowered ceramic items belonging to the Whitaker family. A showpiece of the collections belonging to the archaeologist Sabatino Moscati, that should respect a geographic criterion, is the statue of the Giovinetto with the tunic dress, founded in 1979. Also beautiful is the room with the votive stele and coloured glass, as well as the tool collection and period jewels.

Tel. 0923712598

Opening: from 9 a.m. to 1 p.m. and from 3 p.m. until dusk

king 09237813111), set up by Vincenzo Florio that arrived in Sicily in 1833 and started the production of the Marsala wine in competition with the English producers. Second stop is the Baglio of the Hopps family, along the provincial road 188 towards Salemi. It is a management farm, near the cellars where white, red and Marsala wines are produced. The English family came here at the end of the 18th century as well as John Woodhouse the inventor of the Sicilian and Madeira wine. Following the panoramic provincial road 188 that winds up the vineyards and the hills, you can get to Salemi, Arab city and luxuriant art centre under the Jesuits. A must-see is the impressive castle, the Holy House with the 18th-century frescos and the Civic Museum. Make a stop to the wine bar Sorsi d'Autore (Tel. 0934982485) open at weekends in the almost undamaged old town with alleys and well-kept buildings.

On the 19th of March, for Saint Joseph, the old town gets ready for the festival of the bread. Real jewels made of pasta form decorations and altars. Drive back to the highway from Mazara, few kilometres

03

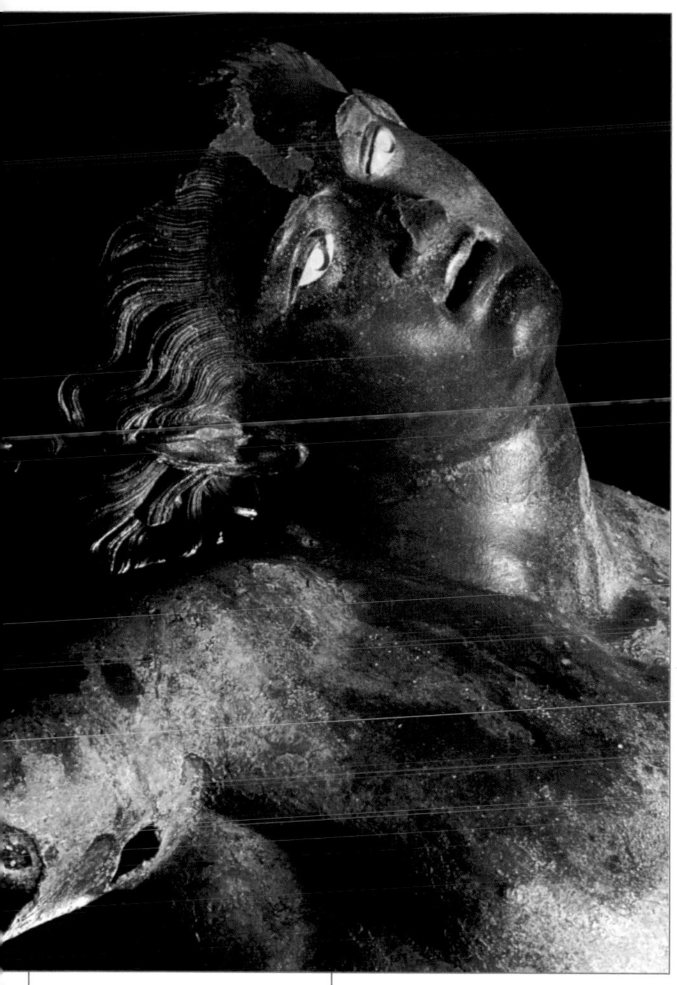

On the left the salt worked at the Ettore and Infersa saltpans, in the top the Satyr kept inside the Church of S. Egidio in Mazara del Vallo

beyond Campobello and you will get to the wide archaeological area of Selinunte. The archaeological park, during the first warm signs that announce that spring has arrived, becomes a breathtaking beauty, for its flowering fields and the temples that slowly slope down towards the coast and the sea. Along the way, make a quick stop to visit the quarry of Cusa, big ancient site from where the columns of the temples of Selinunte were quarried. ■

SPEND THE NIGHT
RESORT KEMPINSKI

It is one of the hundreds hotels plunged in the silence of the planet and not only for its high technology. It is the first resort Kempinski, placed in Mazara del Vallo, Sicilian door on Africa. A huge park among vineyard hills far as the eye can see, interrupted only by old yards where the wine has been produced for centuries.

The silence, the African light, the air mixed with the sea salt brought by the wind, the smell of the land and the must. Just 4 kilometres away there is the crystal-clear sea abounding in fish of the coast of Mazara with its small village of fishermen Capo Granitola with the sea point dedicated to the guests of the resort "Lido di Costanza".

The building of the resort, built in a 19th-century style with Moorish influences, follows the style of the near Baglio Fontanasalsa.

85 suites, all with wide private terraces overlooking the swimming pool or the gazebo in Eastern style that makes you feel like relaxing and meditate before dusk.

On the inside it shows a luxury but never exaggerated style and a genuinely Arabian café with big pillows on stone sofas.

The Spa "Giardino di Costanza", run by Daniela Steiner, suggests special anti-aging and anti-stress treatments made of local products such as salt, clay and citrus fruit.

Address: via Salemi km 7, 100 Mazara del Vallo

Tel. 0923 675000

TRAPANI

THE PROCESSION OF THE "MYSTERIES"

In Trapani, for the Easter week, all the workers, for over 400 years, have brought to the religious procession with the holy stations of the Via Crucis, the Mysteries, twenty sculptural works of art carried out between the XVII and the 18th century. The statues, perfectly kept in the Church of the Purgatorio, are all decorated with old silverware and floral arrangements; they go out for the procession of the Friday afternoon for the long night characterized by the crowd and the traditional "annacata" wave-like movement beat with the notes of the band.

It is the city of the coral, the salt and the harbour with its spectacular boulevard along the medieval walls overlooking the Aegadian Islands. Trapani is a sunny city rediscovered on the occasion of the Vuitton Cup by the sailing world. It is popular for its surrounding area between beaches and promontories, from the Saline to Valderice. The small old town has to be visited by walking along via Garibaldi that still keeps the old typical basolato*1 of Trapani. Along the way you can see the eighteenth-century aristocratic residences such as Palazzo Ricci Morana and Palazzo Fardella. Once you cross via Torrearsa make a stopover to the Fardelliana library shop with its entrance in via S. Agostino. In the old rooms of the former church of San Giacomo, collections of prints, illuminated manuscripts and engravings are kept.

In via Garibaldi, in front of the historical building of the Banco di Sicilia (bank), there is a nice café called Caffè Ra Nova where you can stop, have a drink or an appetizer at the open-air tables just outside the café. A must-see is the Pepoli museum in via Conte Pepoli where you can make a plunge in the sacred art. It contains famous goldsmith's art collections and hundreds of coral items that testify the craft resource of the city among crucifixes, cameos, frontals and late 17th-century cribs. Always in via Pepoli, you can see the Sanctuary of Maria Annunziata, rearranged in the baroque period; it includes 500 masterpieces. Behind the main altar, there is the ivory simulacrum of the Venerable Virgin that the inhabitants of Trapani cover with votive offerings. Still walking on the main street via V. Emanuele peep into the pastry shop windows. One of the most popular is the pastry shop Culicchia, renowned for its crushed-ice drinks. No less charming are the pottery items showed into the craft shops. At the end of via Torre di Ligny, you will come out on the coast, with its eighteenth-century tower transformed today in a museum dedicated to the prehistory and the sea. In order to eat good fish near the ex market retail (that today moved to the fishing harbour), go to Taverna Paradiso (Tel. 092322303), the main course is the couscous but also pasta with shellfish. If you want to buy some tuna fish you can go to the shop Il Tonno in via Isolella, (Tel. 0923557726). If you want to enjoy the night, go to the 8 e mezzo pub in via Palmerio Abate or to the wine bar Per...bacco in via G.B. Fardella. If you want to dance go to the Up&Down disco in via Marsala. ■

On the left, a view of corso Vittorio Emanuele, on the right the Cathedral and the city harbour

*1 Type of road paving stone made with big irregular stones got from the eruptive rocks.

Piazza Armerina,
the entrance of the Casale
Roman residence

04 INNER SICILY BETWEEN ARCHAEOLOGY AND BAROQUE

The inner part of Sicily, dominated by the wheat, is unknown even though it keeps several archaeological jewels. From the city centres of Enna and Caltanissetta to the big and small masterpieces of the baroque period it is a continuous succession of extraordinary landscapes dominated by the hills of the Erean tableland

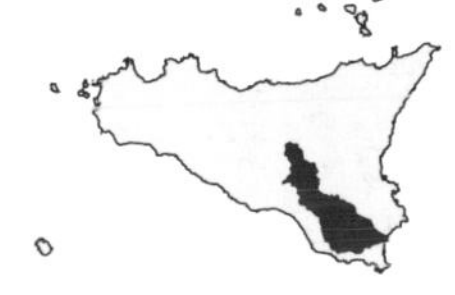

Among vineyards and olive groves, the wavy hills follow one another all covered with wheat as far as the boundary of the surrounding mountains. The Madonie at the back, the river Salso at east, the Erean Mountains and the Nebrodi at south and the Etna on the background: that is the inner part of Sicily.

It is worth to stop for a couple of hours in Morgantina. You can get there from the highway 117 taking the crossroads to Aidone, you cannot miss the small archaeological museum. Going back towards piazza Armerina, situated on the top of the Erean Mountains, after 700 metres you will find the medieval centre. The Arab city was very flourishing under Fredrick II. There, among the alleys of the centre, the Palio dei Normanni is celebrated. It is a commemoration in period costumes from the 12th to the 14th of August. By car, the city seems to be dominated by the Aragonese Castle and by the 17th-century Dome. The city is known for the Roman Villa of the Casale, two km from the built-up area. The villa was re-opened after the restoration; it has four big central bodies decorated with spectacular mosaics in the inside. If you want to visit it you better choose the coolest hours of the day. The visit lasts at least one hour and a half and at the entrance, on require, there are qualified guides. If you want to spend the night

A SITE YOU CANNOT MISS

Morgantina

In a strategic position between Enna, Catania and Syracuse, the old city of the Sicilian king Morges is one of the most extraordinary and less crowded archaeological sites of the island. It was populated since the protohistoric period, first under the Greeks and later under the Romans. The discovery and the excavations started in 1955 and were done by a team of the University of Princeton. A must-see is the terraced citadel at east with the Greek settlement, the mighty boundary wall, the agora, the necropolis, the public buildings and the theatre, seat of classic scenes during summer. You cannot miss a visit at the museum Aidone that will welcome the renowned Venus. (Tel. 093587307 open from 9 a.m. to 6 p.m.)

In the top on the left, the old town centre of Piazza Armerina, on the right the yard of the holiday farm Gigliotto. Here, the prickly pear and pomegranate jelly

at piazza Armerina, there is a wide range of B&B in the old town. At the entrance of the town there is Villa Trigona, a 19th-century charming residence with its delightful 15 rooms (Tel. 093568189). There are also the new high-quality holiday farms with a great gastronomy such as the Vecchia Masseria (Tel. 0935684003), or the Masseria Mandrascate (Tel. 0935375261) between piazza Armerina and Enna. In the farm Torre di Renda (Tel. 0935687657) in summertime you can have lunch on the terrace overlooking the old city and the baroque Dome. You cannot miss, at the entrance of the town, along the highway 117, a gastronomic stopover at Al Fogher, former railway castle with comfortable and warm rooms, fireplace area, name of Veneto, reassessed Sicilian cooking made of hunting provisions, mushrooms, meat and vegetables but also a selected choice of fish (Tel. 0935684123).

You can visit Leonforte at dusk in order to admire the monumental 17th-century fountain open on the hill landscape. There is also a recent and impressive hotel with a spa around a perfectly restored historical residence, Villa Gussio Nicoletti (Tel. 0935903268).

Here, the old oil mill
on the right, the monumental
stairs of Caltagirone

SPEND THE NIGHT IN CALTAGIRONE

Tre metri sopra il cielo
Address: via Bongiovanni 72, along the Scala di S. Maria del Monte
Tel. 09331935106 / 3925686121
Rates: rooms from 60 to 80 euros

La pilozza infiorata
Address: via S.S Salvatore 97
Tel. 093322162 / 3287029543
Rates: rooms from 65 to 75 euros

Driving on the highway 117, in the middle of hundreds of hectares of olive groves, vineyards and prickly pear trees, at the crossroads to Gigliotto you can get to the holiday farm that has the same name (Tel. 0933970898). Go also visit the ancient 13th-century monastery, it has 14 rooms with a view on the old yard or on the pool, you can spend the night there among the silence and the smell of the countryside, you can walk on the several paths and experience the insuperable tastes of the homemade cooking.

In 13 kilometres you can get to Caltagirone, among bends that wind into the several rows of prickly pears that you can pick from October to November. The city has Arabian origins as suggested by the name "castello delle grotte o dei vasi" (castle of the caves and the pots). Under the Normans and the Swabian rules it was a very rich city for the production of the ceramic and still today it counts 200 potteries. After the earthquake

of the 1693 a careful reconstruction was necessary. It was made by the leading Sicilian architects of the period. Leave your car near the Church of San Giacomo, patron of the city, and walk along via V. Emanuele until you get to the city salon, the city hall and the 19th-century Gallery named after don Luigi Sturzo, native of Caltagirone and expert in political affairs. It was also the mayor from 1905 to 1920. Inside the recently restored Gallery you can find shops, bars and the information point. Few steps from there, you will see the big atelier of the master ceramist Riccardo Varsallona in a beautiful liberty-style building with a spectacular exhibition of chandeliers, holy-water stoups, 18th-century majolica objects with cobalt blue, copper green and yellow-orange ornaments on a light background. We are near the stairs of S. Maria del Monte, impressive work of art in lava stone built in the 17th century with 142 steps and redecorated in the 19th century with some tiles describing, like in a trip, the history of the majolica. That is the stage for the most important events of the city such as the Luminaria on the 24th and 25th of July with

A SITE YOU CANNOT MISS

The Casale Roman Villa

Out of the medieval city on a sweet valley, you can find the greatest proof of the Roman Empire in Sicily. The villa was built between the end of the 3rd century and the beginning of the 4th century with a spa belonging to it. Very popular are the mosaics and the ornamental floors with the scene of the ten girls in bikini and the animal pictures made in the Constantinian period.

Tel. 0935687667 - 3392657640

Opening: everyday 10 to 7 p.m.

SPEND THE NIGHT IN CHIARAMONTE GULFI

Villa Zottopera

In Villa Zottopera, 15 minutes by car from Chiaramonte Gulfi, there is an 18th-century farm that belongs to the family Rosso. It is surrounded by 30 hectares of ancient plants; there, the oil has been produced for centuries. The extra-virgin olive oil of Villa Zottopera can be found in few wine bars of the northern Italy and Sicily. The villa, plunged among carob, mulberry and very old prickly pear trees, offers five quiet apartments got from the stables. They have been recently restored with two or three accommodations, wide bathrooms and private terraces on the garden or on the big central yard; they all have the kitchen.

Address: district Roccazzo Chiaramonte Gulfi (RG)

Tel. 3356633052

Rates: B&B 40 euros per person half board 60 euros

a repeat performance in August and the Infiorata in May. If you want to spend the night looking at a view on the old town and on the several churches' steeples (about 50), you can go to the small B&B having the emblematic name "A tre metri sopra il cielo" (Three metres on the heaven), it only has 3 rooms with small terraces on the roof. Near piazza Municipio make a gastronomic stopover at Nonsolovino, you can try its good and reasonably priced Sicilian cooking (Tel. 093331068). Another stop you cannot miss in the city centre is the Church of Gesù in via degli Studi, a late 16th-century structure with the convent of the Jesuits that is part of it. It was the seat of the first universities of Sicily where it was possible to admire some of the works of art of the Caravaggio school (open only during the Mass). On the back, beyond piazza Innocenzo Marcen, you can see the church with its monastery of the Cappuccini Nuovi. Take a relaxing walk in the Villa Comunale designed by Filippo Basile at the beginning of the century. There, you can find specimens of monumental and exotic plants and also ceramic items, copies of pots and panels placed into the green.

From Caltagirone to Chiaramonte Gulfi

Leave Caltagirone and take back the highway and then the freeway towards Ragusa. The landscape becomes softer and almost entirely covered with vineyards. This is the most intensive production area of the Nero d'Avola wine. The vineyards seems

Typical rural landscape of Ragusa, on the right a detail of the baroque style in the old town of Modica

04

to be interspersed by big olive groves that produce a very good and round-shaped Hyblean olive, from where you can get one of the best extra-virgin olive oil of the international market. It is dense and very tasty. If you want to buy it and try the great countryside cooking of Ragusa, make a stop to the farm Zottopera. You can get there by passing the district Fegotto, and the district of Catania and Ragusa towards the crossroads of Vittoria and then following the road signs that bring to the district Roccazzo. From there, there are just 10 kilometres among the fields before you get to the built-up area of Chiaramonte Gulfi up on a hill. In this beautiful medieval district, in the third weekend of November there is the olive oil festival. A must-see, among the city museums, is the Sfilato that is the Sicilian lace in the core of the old town, also open at weekends. Next to the baroque Dome, stop to Mayore, in via Martiri Ungheresi 12 (Tel. 0932928019), it is an old restaurant renowned for its pork-meat homemade cooking. You can buy the pork meat aspic, the local salami and the pork meat, fresh sausages seasoned with fennel and paprika, and the

In the top, some dry walls of the Hyblean landscape. Below the fountain of Hercules in the old town centre

A MUSEUM YOU CANNOT MISS

Museum of the pottery in Caltagirone

The entrance is in the 18th-century theatre inside the city residence in via Roma. There are seven rooms in a modern area gathering all the production of the Sicilian pottery especially the one of the ceramist families Sciacca, Burgio, Trapani, Collesano and Caltagirone.

The works of art, starting from the Middle Ages, include the so-called earthenware figurines. The most famous ones come from the shop of Bongiovanni Vaccaro of the 19th century and represent some scenes of the country life.

Address: via Roma

Tel. 093321680

Opening: 9 to 6.30 p.m. every day

"soppressata" (Italian dry-cured salami). Noteworthy is also the cellar where you can taste, among the 500 labels the Cerasuolo di Vittoria. Few kilometres away from the built-up area of Roccazzo, there is the cellar Poggio di Bortolone, among the various labels, excellent is the red wine Contessa Costanza.

Val di Noto, a journey into the journey

The recognition of the Unesco and the consequent inclusion of Caltagirone, Militello Val di Catania, Catania, Modica, Noto, Palazzolo Acreide, Ragusa Ibla and Scicli, among the "baroque cities of Val di Noto" imposes to visit this area considering it as a journey into the journey.

Important archaeological and historical areas are concentrated within few kilometres; there is Noto Antica, Kasmenai, Avola Antica, Castelluccio and the several small rocky Byzantine churches with frescos all over the area, that make it a place of continuous and strong evocative power for its huge variety of beautiful landscapes. You can go to the Hyblean area between Palazzolo, Avola, Noto and Rosolini where a gorgeous prehistoric canyon winds along the paths of Cassibile and Man-

The Cathedral of ragusa Ibla, on the right the Circolo di Conversazione

SPEND THE NIGHT IN RAGUSA

The Locanda Don Serafino

The scenery is always Hyblean; the hotel is in the old town of Ragusa in a small 19th-century perfectly restored building. It has ten elegant and comfortable rooms, only 22 beds, suitable for those who are looking for a particular holiday. Particular like the new restaurant "Locanda Don Serafino", that in the food-and-wine scenery, represents one of the best restaurants of Sicily (Tel. 0932248778). You cannot miss the creative gastronomy of the multi-awarded Ciccio Sultano in the near restaurant Il Duomo (Tel. 0932651265).

Address: via XI Febbraio 15

Tel. 0932220065

Rates: B&B double room from 148 euros

ghisi. Small lakes and rivers offer uncontaminated natural areas, perfect for those who like quiet and silence. In the triangle Noto-Rosolini-Pachino dedicated to the wine, the vineyards with its typical standard growing, design kilometres of beautiful rural scenes, alternated with millstones, carob plantations, olive and almond groves, agaves, prickly pears and dwarf palms. All around, there are the characteristic dry walls of the Sicilian countryside tradition. As the Unesco called it "the European Capital of the Baroque", Noto can be reached by car from the highway 287. There, all the buildings, churches, monasteries, squares and fountains are shaped in the soft local white stone, expertly produced in order to take the graceful form of a gorgeous stone garden in a unique style. The main streets go from east to west so that the sun can always light them up. After the 1693 earthquake that devastated the entire valley and the cities, Noto was re-built like it was a scenery, by studying and changing the perspective, by playing with the lines and the bending of the facades, with the decoration of the brackets, the scrolls and the volutes, the masks, the puttos, the sirens, the horses, the balconies with wrought iron parapets bending in rounded shapes.

Around the middle of May, from the main doors of the buildings to the streets and the squares, all the landscape is lighted with colours and visions created by a long natural carpet of petals needed by the artists in

order to form flowers decorations to make a different picture every year. You cannot miss the historic Sicilia café, along corso Vittorio. There, you can taste excellent almond sweets, nougats and fruit preserves.
Now the street shows the lovely valleys studded with white stones, carobs and farmhouses until you get to Ragusa Ibla. The old city dominates from above, and is proud of the spectacular and involving history and art with wisdom and harmony. It is a city where the baroque reigns. The discovery of the city winds among churches, buildings, museums, shops, pastries and good restaurants. Walk around and lose yourself among alleys, stairs and visual enfilades that at night, especially in summer, become public art and meeting places. You can also find good quality pubs and restaurants that the city is actually proud of. Some other enjoyable visits are: the old Church of San Giorgio, with its magnificent portal, the Cathedral of San Giovanni Battista, the dome of San Giorgio with its Gagini's works of art and its 3.368 pipes organ, the Church of Santa Maria dell'Itria, the Churches of Santa Maria delle Scale and Miracoli, the Monastery, the Church of Santa Maria di Gesù, the Church of San Francesco with its Swabian bell tower, the Church of San Vincenzo Ferreri with its 16th-century sundial. The discovery goes on with the historic buildings starting from Palazzo Zacco, one of the most beautiful of the city, where the rococo style freely imposes itself. Nowadays, it is a museum of traditions. There is also the Palazzo Schininà of Sant'Elia, Palazzo Sortino-Trono built above the walls of the old castle, Palazzo Cosentini and Palazzo Bertini with their big heads of

THE **NECROPOLIS** OF PANTALICA

Pantalica from the Arabic "buntarigah" that means cave, is plunged between history and nature. It is the biggest necropolis of the Mediterranean with its 5.000 graves inside artificial caves; for some experts it is also the seat of the ancient Hybla of the Sicilian people. Because of its position, the view of the necropolis is delimitated by two big quarries where the rivers Anapo and Calcinara flow. Walking through the reserve can be very impressive. Particularly important is the Anaktoron (building of the prince). There are two valuable naturalistic areas: Vendicari, near Noto and Cava Grande di Cassibile near Avola with its green waters and natural lakes.

Nicastro, La Rocca and Battaglia. By following the provincial road 25 you can get to Castello di Donnafugata, 20 kilometres from Ragusa. The legend says that the earl Bernardo Cabrera imprisoned the princess Blanche of Navarre but she tried to escape through the galleries that brought to the countryside that surrounds the building. Even so, probably, the name of the castle has Arabian origins. It was built on an old structure of a 13th-century tower. One part of the building, including the tower, dates back to the half of the 18th century. However, the whole building was due to the baron Corrado Arezzo that wanted it to be built one century later by putting in the main facade the beautiful neo-Gothic balcony decorated with elegant trefoil arches. The building is on a 2500 square metres surface and has 122 rooms. Noteworthy are the room of the coats, with frescos and aristocratic insignias of the rich Sicilian families, the room of the mirrors, the music room, the billiard room and the bedroom of the princess of Navarre. An 8 hectares luxury park with big ficus trees and other exotic species surround the castle. On the inside there is a labyrinth, a round small temple, a coffeehouse and some artificial caves.
Take the road E 45 towards Modica, along the capital of the ancient county. Today, it is renowned for the production of chocolate that finds a real sanctuary in the Dolceria Bonajuto in corso Umberto. There, the chocolate is worked according to the old traditions that date back to ages ago. Someone calls it the crib-city, gathered around the valleys, hundreds of churches and two domes. Looking at it, is a sheer bliss of the soul, your eyes will never stop, every stone, every stair and every door tells stories of men, artists and immense aristocratic and clerical heritages. It also offers a great gastronomy. There is the Fattoria delle Torri in an 18th-century building with its traditional recipes (Tel. 0932751286), or the picturesque Torre d'Oriente with its terraces high up above the old town. Among the several buildings of the city, there is the cliff of the castle with Torre dell'orologio, the Church of San Domenico, built at the end of the 14th century and re-built in the 17th century. Among the few buildings rescued from the 1693 earthquake, you can find the small rocky Church of San Nicolò of the late Byzantine period enriched by valuable frescos, the beautiful baroque Church of San Pietro that, together with the Church of San Giorgio, is one of the main churches of the city. The city was troubled by heated rivalries so that it was divided in two parts by a bisecting line, real internal boundary of the city.
And still, you can go visit the several buildings. Among the most impressive there are: Palazzo Tedeschi, Palazzo Manenti and Tommasi with their renowned anthropomorphic brackets, Palazzo Polara and the Portale de Leva with its Chiaramonte style. One of the most beautiful is the 18th-century Palazzo dei Mercedari that to-

Modica, the Church of S. Pietro

A variety of chocolate produced by the Antica Dolceria Bonajuto in Modica

THE **EUROCHOCOLATE** EVENT

In April there is the Eurochocolate in Modica, showcase of the food of the gods. There, the chocolate has a very old origin and peculiar features that make it the only one, pure, simple, with unmistakable flavours thanks to the old Aztec recipe gained with the Spanish rule. The recipe imposes the cold working, the use of the aromas such as the cinnamon, vanilla, lately also paprika, citrus, coffee, carob and much more. Laboratories, tasting, books, music, games, sleepless white and dark nights, combined with wines, food and international competitions liven up the festivals that gathers always more and more visitors.

day hosts the Hyblean museum of popular arts and traditions with its typical perfectly restored craft shops. You cannot forget the 15th-century Church of Santa Maria di Betlem, reconstructed in baroque style but enriched with late Gothic, Arabian, Norman and Catalan features and with a valuable 19th-century earthenware crib. You can also visit the Church of the Carmine, built in 1250 in Siculo-Gorthic style (and partially reconstructed in baroque style) by the Carmelites that, escaped from Palestine, took shelter in the county. Eventually, visit S. Giorgio, the 18th-century Dome of the high city that looks like the Roman S. Trinità dei Monti, the most beautiful example of the Hyblean baroque.

From Modica, driving towards via del Barocco you can get to Scicli, small centre set among three valleys, high rocky walls, gorges and karstic caves.

There, the baroque principles used in the reconstruction and based on the search of illusionistic spaces and effects, got from the expert disposition of the urban map, have created the small jewel that is Scicli today.

Once, it was dominated by the Arabs, later by the Normans, as the Sanctuary of Madonna delle Milizie, 1.5 kilometres from Scicli towards

the coast, reminds us. The visit to the small town can start from piazza Italia where, except for the beautiful 18th-century buildings, such as the former monastic complex Padri Carmelitani and Palazzo Beneventano, you can see the Church Madonna delle Milizie rich in golden stuccoworks and frescos. Driving towards the sea, 8 kilometres from Scicli, visit the town and the castle of Donnalucata. It is a very ancient village and old harbour of Scicli whose name probably comes from the Arabic "Ainlu Kat" that means spring of the hours. According to an Arab observer, it refers to a fountain from where the water used to flow irregularly and just during the Muslim prayer. Some other historians, claim that it refers to a miraculous appearance of the Virgin, when the Arabs, guided by the emir Belcane, landed along the coasts in order to reconquer Sicily, now dominated by the Normans. In that occasion the people of the city asked to the Virgin for help and She appeared covered by a glimmering light. The fresh fish here rules. On this point there are only two names: Al Ghiottone and al Molo restaurant.

In the surroundings, a must-see is the spectacular archaeological area of Pantalica, the biggest of the Mediterranean necropolis with its 5 thousand graves with artificial caves. ■

SPEND THE NIGHT IN VAL DI NOTO

Giardino di Pietra
This 18th-century building has a garden and a wonderful view on the domes of the Cathedral.
Address: via C.Guerra 13
Tel. 0932621809
Rates: double room from 110 to 130 euros

Caelum Hiblae
From every room you can see the dome and the Hyblean countryside.
Address: via Salita Specula 11
Tel. 093222042
Rates: double room from 110 to 130 euros

The Eremo della Giubilana
It looks like a 15th-century monastery. The rooms are enveloped in a dimension that runs out of time.
Address: district Giubiliana, 9, Marina di Ragusa (RG)
Tel. 0932669119
Rates: double room from 110 to 130 euros

Balarte
This place is usually out of the trip itinerary, it keeps the habits of a perfect hospitality.
Address: district Scorrione, Modica (RG)
Tel. 0932779014
Rates: double room from 110 to 130 euros

Talìa
It is a small oasis in the old town. From the entrance you can get to the rooms placed in more tiers.
Address: via Exaudinos 1/9, Modica (RG)
Tel. 0932752075
Rates: double room from 110 to 130 euros

ENNA

THE RELIGIOUS PROCESSION OF THE HOODED BELIEVER

The life of the city is still characterized by the importance of the brotherhoods that liven up the most significant festival of the city: The Procession of the Holy Week that starts on Palm Sunday. In the Dome, the brotherhoods alternate; they start from their churches followed by the band. On Friday night there is the impressive religious procession of the "Incappucciati" (people wearing a hood).

The tower of Fredrick

Spectacular view on the inner part of Sicily, it is the higher Italian provincial capital. Enna was populated since the prehistory. Starting from the central via Roma, pedestrian area on Saturday afternoon, there is a handy parking area near Castello, from there you can plunge in the core of the old town, populated, illuminated and livened-up until night. In the past, Enna was called the city of the towers; there were lots of them, given the defensive attitude of the city. Some of them do not exist anymore, some have been incorporated as bells, into the churches, like the octagonal tower built under Fredrick II of Swabia, situated in a predominant position in the middle of a public garden at the end of via Roma (open from 9 to 5). You can also visit the Dome; it was built in 1307 and reconstructed in baroque style with some sculptures by Gagini and the Castello di Lombardia dating back to the Norman period under Frederick II of Sicily; it was reinforced and decorated with rooms that made it suitable for the court life. Along via Roma you can also find the great part of the monuments but also shops, restaurants and bakers that sell delicious bread made with excellent durum wheat coming from Val Dittaino. The typical cooking of Enna, made of vegetables, can be tasted to the restaurant Centrale in piazzetta IV Dicembre with tables outdoor starting from May. Also the restaurant Belvedere da Gino makes an excellent pizza. Do not forget to taste the local cheese combined with peach marmalade; it is served at the wine bar Belvedere by Christian Augello that also gathers 600 labels of Italian and Sicilian wines. Beyond the Dome, there is the Museum Alessi (open Mon to Fry 8 a.m. to 8 p.m.); it keeps precious ornament collections and 17th and 18th century vestments. They are embroidered with a golden thread and corals; very beautiful is the gold Crown of the Virgin, there is also a picture gallery at the mezzanine where a sweet Madonna and Child by an anonymous Fleming of the 15th century shines. In the second floor, among Greek, Roman and Byzantine coins, you can admire some archaeological finds dating back from the prehistory to the Middle Ages and an interesting collection of Egyptian funerary figurines probably coming from grave outfits. The archaeological museum that has its seat in the nearest Palazzo Varisano (Mon to Fry 9 a.m. to 6.30 p.m.) gathers several finds, especially earthenware, coming from the necropolis of Calascibetta and Capodarso. Taking via Polizzi and then turning on the right, you can find the Chiesa del SS. Salvatore in via del Salvatore, a 16th-century reworking of an ancient recently restored basilian church. In piazza Colajanni, sociologist from Enna, you can see the Church of Santa Chiara with its majolica floor.■

CALTANISSETTA

The core of the old town, almost a baroque salon, is piazza Garibaldi dominated by the dome and the facade of the Cathedral of Santa Maria. On the other side of the square, with the statue of Triton in the middle, there is another beautiful facade of a baroque church dedicated to St. Sebastian that saved the city from the plague. Caltanissetta, whose name comes from the Arabic "castle of the women" sprang up around the Saracen castle of Pietrarossa and developed under the Normans and the Angevins. The old town can be visited in few hours; during Easter it becomes a real theatre of the Miracle Play of the Holy Week with the processions on the Holy Wednesday, Thursday and Friday.
Take a walk in corso Umberto I, leaving behind the city hall or Palazzo del Carmine and the adjoining theatre Regina Margherita, and among the baroque facades you can get to the Church of Sant'Agata al Collegio, built by the Jesuits with wonderful marble works of art placed in the interior. Do not miss the puttos by Marabitti and the altar of Sant'Ignazio with marble polychromatic inlaid works; it is a real baroque jewel with floral and birds patterns. The building of the Colleggio, belonging to the church, is today a city library with a big open-air hall available for cultural events. On the left, make a stopover to the Gran Café Romano between the most renowned pastry shops and meeting places. It is the perfect place to eat fried arancini and local desserts that you can also find in the new Pasticceria d'Autore. The city boasts a real leadership in the production of almond and pistachio nougats; the oldest laboratory, dating back to 1870, produces and sells by retail. You can find it in front of the railway station in via Pulci. Along salita Matteotti, few metres from the city hall, hidden among the buildings of the lords of the sulphur, there is the 17th-century Palazzo Moncada, mighty square baroque structure decorated with anthropomorphic sculptures. Always in piazza Garibaldi, in an alley, there is the new restaurant for real gourmets, the Vicolo Duomo (Tel 0934582331). You can taste their excellent appetizers and main courses of the old Sicilian gastronomy. Before you enter the medieval alleys of the so-called district Angeli, make a visit to the small bookshop of the publisher Sciascia that in the 60s was the core of the cultural life of the entire district. Along via S. Domenico, beyond the late 15th-century church that has the same name, you can walk up until the ruins of Castello di Pietrarossa. If you want to spend the night in a charming place you can go to the new B&B Antichi Ricordi, it has a beautiful indoor yard in via villa Glori, 45 (Tel. 3384910905). ■

THE HOLY WEEK AND THE SIXTEEN "VARE"

In Caltanissetta, there are 16 statuary groups reminding the pictures of the Passion. They parade in the Procession on the Holy Thursday through the streets of the old town until dusk. On the Holy Friday, heartfelt is the Procession of the "Vare", emblematic groups of the Via Crucis that liven up the afternoon according to an old ritual that involves both Arts and Skills. You cannot miss the Holy Friday of the near village Pietraperzia, where at dusk, a spectacular representation is repeated. It takes an emblematic name "Lu Signuri di li Fasci" (in Sicilian dialect means God of the bands) from the real scenery signed by the movement of the long white linen bands brought by the believers and placed in circles around a huge trunk.

The fountain of Neptune and the Cathedral

The Scala dei Turchi
of Realmonte
in the province of Agrigento

THE AFRICAN COAST THE SECRET BEACHES OF THE TV SERIES OF MONTALBANO

It is a trip for those who are in search of the last ribbon of uncontaminated sea and quiet villages, well known because of the tv series of Montalbano, where you can rediscover the old traditions and new lifestyle

Flat and infinite beaches: they could be uncomfortable, steep, white, yellow or even black. Those who are looking for a secret sea spot have to be ready for a real treasure hunt. You better make your way towards the beaches of Ragusa or Agrigento. They have recently been discovered by the TV sets but you can always find a quiet place to dive to the open sea in front of Africa where the sea still smells like salt and seaweed and not like fuel and suntan cream.

There are kilometres of dunes carved by the wind where only the self-sown vegetation grows up and also very long white sand areas streach, with some yellow and ochre spots interrupted by some bays, islets, promontories, castles, towers, fishing nets and fishing villages. Here the sun sets slowly while the sea becomes red like wine. This show can only last for a couple of hours. It is the light that tells you that you are on a strip of land of the south of Europe, few steps from Africa. This is the rough, dry and bare Sicily of the TV series out of the Andrea Camilleri novels with his literary places with precise geographical similarities that are the background to the series of Montalbano. This part of Sicily is not very popular; it stretches beyond the places we can only imagine and covers an entire pro-

In the top the fishermen of Sampieri, next to it the beach of Cala Mosche, below the natural reserve of Vendicari

vince of the southeast area that from Syracuse arrives to the coasts of the Pirandellian Agrigento.

Cala delle Mosche and Vendicari

In the core of Ragusa you can find carob, almond and olive groves interrupted by the white stone structures.
Follow the road signs to get to Noto-Pachino, the natural reserve of Vendicari that with its five brackish swamps is a charming place in any season. From the main entrance of the reserve you can get to the sea by walking around the wonderful Mediterranean vegetation characterized by the wind and the sea salt. Once, the swamps were used as saltpans, while the big fishing net, rising above the Swabian sighting tower, was abandoned in the 40s.
Surrounded by heathers, junipers and tamarisks you can get to Cala delle Mosche, almost a strip of Africa. A light green bed of reeds stands on what had to be a mouth of a river; the yellow rock eaten away by the wind frames a strip of white sand desert that flows in the blue sea. Surprising is the depth of the

In the top the tunny-fishing area of Marzamemi, on the right, the house of Vitaliano Brancati

beach, the light sand, the transparent water full of amberjacks, grey mullets and white sea breams that can only be seen in few islands. For those who can smell the seaweed and observe some tricks of the light between rocks and sea, the thought flies to the Isola dei Conigli in Lampedusa, protected seaside area where the turtles nest.

The few refreshment areas at the entrance of the island only offer something to drink and some shadow under the carob trees. A very good holiday farm, for its position, is the restored cottage La Corte del Sole, a 19th-century manor with a wide white stone yard and a pool.

Marzamemi

Driving towards the sea village of Marzamemi, the beaches are one after the other: the crowded San Lorenzo and the larger Spinazza that surround the crystal-clear sea of the gulf of Noto. A small bar, beach umbrellas and deckchairs are placed at the gates of the old fishing village lately used as set by the TV fictions. Here, an open-air film fe-

SPEND THE NIGHT NEAR THE BEACH

La Corte del Sole Eloro
Address: district Bucachemi - Noto Marina - Eloro (SR)
Tel. 0931820210
Rates: 40-50 euros per person

Il Roveto
Old restored farm of the 17th-century, offers comfortable apartments with a private yard.
Address: district Roveto Vendicari (SR)
Tel. 093166024 - 3394123148
Rates: 35 euros per person

Houses for rent by the fishing nets
Ago Sud Agency
Apartment with a view on the sea or on the fishing area of Marzamemi (SR)
Address: via Randazzo 34 (CT)
Tel. 3471167865
Rates: 34 euros per person

stival and village fairs are held in the last week of July. The obligatory subjects are sea and food, the tomatoes of the near Pachino and the tuna fish botargo.
Marzamemi, with its 18th-century small church that stands on the stone square includes the restored quick-stone body today turned into simple apartments for rent. The houses, with their old countryside Sicilian furniture, sleeping lofts and kitchen areas, all enjoy the breathtaking view.
There is the Casa Bruno with a small backyard that stands on the harbour or the Casa del Principe set against the old church with a beautiful terrace on the roof. A bar called Cialoma, like the song of the fishermen, and other meeting places give you the chance to enjoy the sight of the square. There are also two ethnic shops in the yard manor belonging to the princes of Villadorata that show fanciful jewels, the Nero d'Avola wine and the chocolate from Modica until night-time.
Further on, along via Marzamemi, there is the holiday farm of Paolo and Cristina Campisi that has cooked the seafood for five generations. The father, Salvatore, used to dry in the sun the eggs of the amberjacks and tuna

fish; that is how the popular botargo is made and used by the best Italian chefs. On the external wall of the building there is the picture that shows the technique of the tuna slaughter: there is the room of the death that stands between Marzamemi and Portopalo di Capo Passero, and the other big fishing net that proves the fate of this strip of Sicily in the beginning of the century, before the farming and the tourism boom. There, you cannot miss the dried in-oil tomatoes from Pachino, the pâté and the tomato concentrate. At night try the food tasting and then follow the sunset by sitting on the stones of the dam that overlooks the Lido Spinazza. Make a stop to Celeste (via Del Porto 7, Tel. 0931841244), small family hotel on the beach in front of the house of Vitaliano Brancati that stands on the water as if by magic. In a small room that overlooks the sea, you can taste the fish couscous of the good old days, the Tunisian recipe is by the chef Fathi; it is made of semolina worked by expert hands and an insuperable soup with fresh fish (depending on what the sea offers): groupers, scorpion fish, teleost fish, lobsters, but also vegetables, aubergines, courgettes, peppers and potatoes. At the end, try the wonderful coffee or the crushed-ice drinks flavoured with watermelon, mulberry, almond and prickly pear, made by the bar Pagoda served on tables on the beach. People also have it for breakfast; this tradition could also be concluded with a big brioche filled with whipped cream.

Almond and mulberry water ice together with the popular brioches, on the right a view of the coast of Ragusa

SPEND THE NIGHT NEAR THE RIVER

Resort Donnalucata

If you want to spend the night at few kilometres away from the reserve, by breathing the sea smell and the spring flowers try this new four stars resort. It stands in an old quick-stone nightclub. It is a real oasis of relax where comfort and elegance are ensured. The most panoramic rooms are in the second floor all gathered around the pool and overlooking the Syracuse sea near the entrance of the reserve. It also has a small wellness centre.

Address: provincial road 63 Scicli (RG)

Tel. 0932850286

THE MOUTH OF THE **RIVER IRMINIO** WITHIN A WOOD

It is a heaven of nature hidden among the dunes and the wood, along the highway between Marina di Ragusa and Donnalucata. Here, the longest river of Ragusa, after 50 kilometres of flowing the Hyblean tableland, gets to the sea creating a wonderful landscape, a habitat where the birds can find a safe shelter. The fresh water seeps among the sea salt-resistant plants that grow up on the sand and huge bushes of lentisk and ancient juniper that thrown down by the wind form a real tunnel thick like wood. Walking through the silence only broken by the sound of the sea, along the bank of the river, you can notice the classic plants of the waterways: the ditch reed, the bulrush and the tamarisk. Here we are in the special reserve of the mouth of the river Irminio, in Ragusa between Scicli and Marina di Ragusa. The shape of the mouth changes like a map according to the flow of the water and the force of the sea that knock down huge trunks where cormorants, seagulls and little egrets stay. The special reserve of the mouth of the river Irminio is actually a strip of primitive nature that brings the visitor back in time until ancient periods, when the man used to sail the watercourse and boost trade, as shown by the nearest archaeological area. The river was definitely used as a ca-

A view of the district of Sampieri, on the right the typical landscape of the dunes on the sea

Beach of Sampieri

It is hard to notice the beauty of the dry-stone walls, the yellow fields, the carob and prickly pear trees and the sea when you go from Syracuse to Ragusa. From Portopalo, by following the seaside street towards Borgo Sampieri and Donnalucata you will be surprised by the beaches that stretch for a few dozen kilometres. Cava d'Aliga, in the district Pisciotto, is another set loved by Zingaretti (actor of the TV series Montalbano). We are in Scicli, where the sea is often choppy because of the light breeze, the African hot weather is intolerable and the lifeguards work until dusk. Here, the sand is extremely soft to the touch and frames the beach with very high dunes. Sampieri is not really crowded except for the weekends of late in August. You can even play bowls or tamburello in the wide sandy shore lashed by the sea, but be careful do not trip over the near beach towel.

Marina di Ragusa

It is now a renowned beach, almost a small local Santa Monica. Full of palms from Morocco, families riding bikes, music, appetizers and corpulent surfers attracted by the wind of the channel. One shore after the other and you get to the town that stands under the Spanish tower and the quay frangiflutti. In

nal harbour and boundary with the near Camarina. At the beginning of the century it looked like a wide marsh between Marina di Ragusa and Plaja Grande, it was reclaimed and subject to several deforestations along the watercourse used to irrigate the farming of the area.
Today, the reserve is well organized and has a security service that guarantees a careful and respectful fruition. 130 hectares divided in zone A and zone B, a visiting centre inside a beautiful stone cottage that also hosts a small museum of the surrounding flora and fauna. A big bird inside a window at the entrance of the museum welcomes the visitors; it was killed by the poachers and found by the security guards among the dunes. It is now the symbol of an aggression on nature that has to be fought with good rules and respectful principles that today put the life of the protected area in order.
4 of the paths are open to the public; mostly pupils committed in environmental education projects together with the provincial offices of the reserve, or tourists and naturalist experts attracted by the spectacular flora of the dunes. The path Gelso goes under the street in order to reach the river and the mouth among very high ditch reeds and lentisk groves; the other two paths start from the entrance at the boundary of the reserve. "This is one of the most important issue for those who guarantee the protection of the environment" as explained by the naturalist Maria Di Maio, director of the reserve managed by the Province of Ragusa. "The bathers, but also the excursionists, if in great numbers, can modify the delicate balance of flora and fauna".
"The car transit and the loading and unloading in the water are risky factors, but now, our attention goes to the activity of divulgation, environmental education and research; soon the herbarium will be open to the public as well as the museum that will be addressed to all the European experts".

the 50s, the high-society of Ragusa, used to go there to spend the day to the sea of Serafino; they used to start with a wonderful fish soup. The recipe is always the same and is served in the oldest shore of the area. It is a white and blue wooden structure, two terraces, tables strictly set with white tablecloths, a big room used in winter and few bathing huts all around. At dusk you cannot miss the wonderful terrace of the new restaurant Baciamolemani, modern design, 400 Sicilian wine labels, blue lights and a huge white sofa where you can sink and look at the horizon. At Baciamolemani (promenade Andrea Doria 21, Tel. 0932615720) is impossible to have dinner without a reservation, not even the great pizza with caciocavallo cheese from Ragusa and tomatoes from Pachino. The owners, two young men of Ragusa, passionately fond of cooking, started it for fun. They serve raw fish appetizers, local vegetables combined with Nero d'Avola and Sicilian white wines; reinvented cooking made of fresh fish of the near marines.

From Torre Salsa to the mouth of the river Belice

If we exclude the beach of Punta Secca, near Siculiana Marina in the province of Agrigento, white lonely sandy shore where Montalbano used to meet his reliable friend Gegé, the real queen of the totemic charm is the so-called "Scala dei Turchi" for its extraordinary ochre-white chalky architecture hollowed out by the wind and the waves.

It is an incredible succession of natural steps alternated with white sand and rocky coves that overlook the cold and clean sea at the gates of Agrigento near Realmonte.
In order to make a very special gastronomic stopover and enjoy a panoramic view on the countryside with the temples lighted at dusk, you cannot miss the terraced restaurant of the hotel Baglio della Luna (Tel. 0922511061), situated inside an 18th-century restored sighting tower. The multi-awarded chef makes very sophisticated dishes, almost exclusively made of fish. Only 15 kilometres from Templi, beyond the Capo di Siculiana, you will see the infinite sand oasis that in the eastern point takes the name of Torre Salsa. The reserve managed by

WWF guaranteed that the natural environment and the cold crystal-clear water teeming with fish today is still one of the most undamaged Sicilian areas. Here you can find different habitats: sand, dunes, lake areas with the mouth of the river Salso, natural Mediterranean spot 6 kilometres long. You cannot miss at dusk a bath and a romantic dinner. Towards Marinella di Selinunte, down to the pinewood, leave your car at the gates of the Foce del Belice reserve and admire kilometres of desert

On the left Porto Palo, Isola di Capo Passero, above, the dunes of the natural reserve of Torre Salsa, below, the Scala dei Turchi

05

On the left, the nature and the uncontaminated sea of the reserve Torre Salsa, above, the typical fishing boats of Ragusa

beach bordered by the African dunes. A hundred kilometres from the sea there is a wooden ladder illuminated by the torches that brings to the sand where you will find a dozen of tables next to a small private lido. We are just few kilometres away from the archaeological park of Selinunte.■

SIRACUSA

A MUSEUM YOU CANNOT MISS

Paolo Orsi Museum

The museum is situated in the expansion areas of the city inside the park of Villa Landolina. It is rich in vestiges (Christian hypogeum, pieces of ancient necropolis, elements of the Hellenistic built-up area of Syracuse). It shows history and prehistory of almost all the eastern and central Sicily archaeological sites, until the end of the classic age.

Address: viale Teocrito 66 (SR)
Tel. 0931464022
Opening: from Tue to Sat 9 a.m. to 7 p.m.
Sunday and holiday 9 a.m. to 1 p.m.
Closed on Monday

Ortygia, baroque heart of the Greek Syracuse, during summer becomes a small Paris with cafes, pubs, yards and terraces livened up until late at night. In the big stone theatre, a few kilometres from the island, the Greek rite of the classical tragedy takes place in May. It is a regular appointment for international culture. In July instead, the harbour called Porto Grande di Siracusa and the seat of the Italian Navy League become a meeting point of impressive races.

Ortygia, an island-labyrinth among alleys, yards and buildings, has on one side the promenade where during summer wooden platforms with wide solariums, deckchairs and beach umbrella are placed; on the other side there is a big harbour with an imposing group of moored boats and sailing ships. The island is connected to Syracuse by a bridge and once you get past it you will not find any car so you can enjoy the walking and maybe also a fruit or almond water ice. A must-see in the old town of Ortygia is the Castello Maniace, recently restored and open to the public for big events. It is an imposing castle built as bastion of the island and the city, stretching out on a staggering blue seabed. Built by Frederick II with a square plan and four towers in the corners, lighted at night, it is like a boat leaning over the sea breeze. But the hearth of Ortygia is without any doubt the fountain of Arethuse with its papyrus. The legend says that the nymph Arethuse joined up in the water with Artemis that became a river. Here, the big historical hotels built at the beginning of the century, after years of restoration are now open: the Grand Hotel Ortigia (Tel. 0931464600) and the Des Etrangers (0931319100). Beautiful terraces with a panoramic view on the canal harbour and the roofs of the old town are the perfect place for a quite happy hour at dusk.

Piazza Duomo is a real stone sitting room with the facade of the cathedral entirely restored in the half of the 18th-century with two Corinthian order columns. At the entrance, between the naves, you can see the columns of the Temple of Athena built in the 5th century and then turned into a church by the Christians. Inside the Dome you can find wonderful statues of the Sicilian school by Gagini. Take an unusual walk in the hypogeum that in ancient times and still today connects the island to the sea. For those who love art there is the

In the top, the hall of the Cathedral, on the right the basin of Syracuse, in the backgound the buildings of Ortigia

Ristorante

SIRACUSA

THE CLASSICAL REPRESENTATIONS

Appointment for the Sicilian culture: the representations of the Greek theatre are organized by the National Institute of Drama. Aeschylus inaugurated the first cycle of classical performances on The 16th of April 1914 with Agamemnon. From then, the Classical Representations, arrived at the 44th edition, are held in May.
The Greek theatre of Syracuse was built in the 5th century BC.

INDA
Address: corso Matteotti 29 (SR)
Tel. 0931487248
Website:
www.indafondazione.org

interesting museum of Palazzo Bellomo found in a beautiful 15th-century building. There, you can find some sculptures by Laurana and Gagini, paintings by Caravaggio, vestments and valuable silverware of Sicilian handicraft. If you want to spend the night in the town of Ortygia, go to Palazzo del Sale, a perfectly restored 18th-century building with Sicilian antiques and a modern design. Out of the city you can spend the night at the Caol Ishka hotel that lies along the river Ciane. The resort has designer furniture, wide yards, a pool, a wellness centre, a small private solarium along the river and a Mediterranean garden.

Other hotels are Algilà Ortigia Charme Hotel (Tel. 0931465186), a sophisticated old building with a panoramic view on the Ionian Sea in a clean position where swimming is permitted. Renowned are the gastronomic stops to Don Camillo (Tel. 093167133), Minosse (Tel. 093166366) or to the Cantinaccia in via XX Settembre (Tel. 093165945).

Another idea for those who love history is the Miqweh, that is, the Jewish bath of the Byzantine period situated at 18 metres underground, only reachable by a long staircase (Tel. 093122255).

Once you leave Ortygia with its wonderful baroque style and extraordinary streets, the trip goes on towards the Syracuse Latomie, the old calcareous stone caves from where the Greeks used to take the material that was necessary to build temples, streets and defensive walls that now are one of the main attractions of the archaeological heritage of Syracuse. It is a complex system that stretches in the northern part of the Greek city. With the past of the years it was widened starting from the Latomia dei Cappuccini towards west, the Latomie di Novanteri, the Casale, Santa Venera, the Intagliatella and the Paradiso. The Latomia dei Cappuccini is the biggest quarry that, at the end of the 16th century, was included in the nearest and overhanging Monastery of the Capuchin Friars.

The beaches that surround the city give you the chance to spend few hours there without driving so far. You can choose the equipped beaches of Fontane Bianche or the crystal waters of Plemmirio, protected sea area standing along the rocks of the peninsula of the Maddalena. ■

In the top, the entrance of the Cathedral of ortigia. Here, a moment of the picturesque classical representations

SPEND THE NIGHT IN SIRACUSA

Il Palazzo del Sale
18th-century building with Sicilian antiques and a modern design.
Address: via S.Teresa 25
Tel. 093165958
Rates: from 60 to 80 euros

Domus Aurea
Quiet atmosphere in the hotel of the Ursuline nuns of Ortygia.
Address: via V.Veneto 76
Tel. 093124854
Rates: double room 135 euros in B&B

Gutkowsky
Boarding house with sea view and very accurate design.
Address: lungomare Vittorini 26
Tel. 0931465861
Rates: B&B, double room 100 euros

Caol Ishka
Quiet and sophisticated hotel situated along the river Ciane.
Address: via Elorina, district Pantanelli
Tel. 093169057
Rates: double room from 190

L'Approdo delle Sirene B&B
Address: Riva Garibaldi 15
Tel. 093124857
Rates: double room 75 euros

Giuggiulena B&B
Address: via Pitagora da Reggio 35
Tel. 0931468142
Rates: double room 100 euros

The sunset on a boat between Alicudi and Filicudi

06 SMALL ISLANDS NOT JUST ABOUT GLAMOUR

The Minor Islands consist of 13 sea and seabed and treasures. Some of them have been transformed by a pressing tourism, some others are still undamaged: take a trip to the Aeolian and the Aegadian Islands, possibly out of season when the nature is an explosion of colours and perfumes, to Pantelleria, known as the black pearl of the Mediterranean Sea, and to the furthest Pelagie Islands, Lampedusa and Linosa

Aeolian, islands of fire

The archipelago is a universe made up of seas and volcanoes that attract people for its irresistible exoticism. For centuries, nature and history have shaped a landscape sculpted by fire, lava, wind and sea. Nowadays, the Aeolian islands have attracted a large number of tourists for just two months a year, when VIPs, sailing boats, rubber dinghies and dream yachts compete for a place alongside the quay and for a candle light dinner on a private terrace overlooking the archipelago. For the rest of the year, they turn into seven silent paradises, sea patches and enchanted sunsets.

Lipari, the largest island, is the municipal building. It is often very busy because of the presence of the harbour but it is also a destination for archaeology lovers who visit the extraordinary museum inside the Spanish castle that is dedicated to the great scholar, Professor Luigi Bernabò Brea. Stromboli offers a spectacular sight of the active volcano and Salina, the green island, is becoming more and more a destination for yachtsmen.

Panarea, “the lady of the night”, in July and August usually becomes the busiest amusement area that can even be the envy of the Emerald

Coast, but immediately after August 15th, it is almost totally deserted again like Filicudi, the small black pearl, that is full of VIPs and scuba diving lovers, whereas, Alicudi is much further and wilder.

Stromboli, an explosion of lava

The Stromboli volcano's activity has lasted for 2000 years and it leaves people astonished looking up at the frequent explosive eruptions of lapilli, lava and stones that, roll along the stream of fire and plunge directly into the sea. For tourists who come to this island, the eruption is an unavoidable sight which can be seen in different ways: walking for a half-day excursion up to the crater, or on the boat, or waiting for a volcano rumble in dark summer nights. In Ficogrande, overlooking the rock of Strombolicchio, which is brightened up at night, you can feel the breath of the fire at the foot of the active volcano slope. In Stromboli, an oasis of silence and peace, you can walk under the moonlight without any public lighting. The Eos theatre, facing the sunrise, offers movie and theatre shows within the garden of the hotel

In the top, the stacks of Lipari, a view of the pumice stones. Here, Panarea, the rock of Dattilo

Stromboli, some fishermen on the beach; in the background Strombolicchio, on the right the houses of Piscità

La Sirenetta, where you can find 53 comfortable rooms, facing the beaches, with large balconies completely dipped in the green. Another oasis of quiet is the hotel La Sciara, an up-country hotel almost hidden between the white concrete walls and the green belt at the foot of the volcano. It is one of the most ancient hotels of the island, with 62 rooms furnished with old Sicilian and Neapolitan pieces of furniture, a large salt water swimming pool and 5 villas in a residence on the beach not far from the hotel, most of the time, booked by VIPs who want total privacy. Behind the church, at the town's square, you can find the house of Roberto Rossellini and the divine Ingrid Bergman, where they lived during the filming of the movie " Stromboli, terra da Dio". You can even find the pictures of the young and beautiful star in a bar at the square having the same name. Barbablù is a charming inn run by a man from Naples and his wife from Venice, who is very good at dressing bread mixing Mediterranean flavours. Here, you can breath the air of a different time. There are old Aeolian pieces of furniture and antiques, and the hotel rooms are elegant, large

Below on the left, the walking tour around the volcano, on the right the typical three-wheeler in the narrow alleys of Stromboli

and open onto a terrace overlooking the volcano. The cuisine of Stromboli is extremely simple and represents a real taste of the sea, even if there are just few fishermen left in the island. Do not miss a trip to Ginostra where you can find lots of white houses situated along the middle coast of the island. But the dream of the smallest harbour in the world called "pertuso" (hole), where docking is not allowed but landing is permitted, seems to be the same. There are still donkeys helping people to go up to the lava stone steps to reach the city centre, some people who talk in a weird dialect, Mrs. Ingrid who rents rooms and B&B, close to the church, using old Aeolian houses recently restored with their typical arcade, reed roofs and old whitened wells. Here, in summer, you can find insular immigrants who come back from Australia or Argentina. You can even find people looking for a room to rent and hoping to find the last enchanted place far from the massive tourism and the complications of the organized life. Far away from the civilization, you can go up and down the lava steps reaching the sea under the burning sun. At night, you will be satisfied with the world's most spectacular sight. In Ginostra, the electric light has recently arrived and you can see every single Aeolian island that, for some strange reason, seem to be larger; that is why you can lose the count of them.

Salina, a green oasis

When you get to Salina you can admire two green twin towers; it has recently become a protected natural reserve and is the second-largest island after Lipari. It is becoming a fast-growing island managed by three other different towns for geographical reasons. It is famous thanks to the actor Massimo Troisi who played a role on the set of Il Postino, a Neruda movie. He discovered the hidden beauty of Pollara, a small village where some farmers live; it is located at the bottom of an extinct volcano, with a wonderful beach overlooking the sea stacks. We recommend two charming resorts where the simple Aeolian style still exists: the Capo Faro situated between the Malvasia rows and the Signum. It is a small village turned into a hotel, among the houses of Malfa. The Signum was

A glass of Malvasia wine from Salina, the "nectar of the gods", on the right the beach of Pollara renowned because of the movie "Il postino" by Troisi

SPEND THE NIGHT IN SALINA AND STROMBOLI

Capo Faro
Address: via Faro 3
Malfa - Salina
Tel. 0909844330
Rates: from 190 to 420, junior suites double room in B&B, open from Easter to the end of October

Signum hotel and restaurant
Address: via Scalo 15
Malfa - Salina
Tel. 0909844222
Rates: from 110 to 210 euros double room, breakfast included open from mid-March to November, it has a wellness centre

Principe di Salina
Address: via Nazionale 3 Malfa - Salina
Tel. 0909844415
Rates: double rooms from 120 to 200 euros in B&B, open from April to October

L'Ariana
Address: via Rotabile 11 Rinella di Leni - Salina
Tel. 0909809075
Rates: double room in B&B, from 80 euros

La Sirenetta
Address: Ficogrande Stromboli
Tel. 090986025
Rates: double room in B&B, from 120 euros

Locanda Barbablù
Address: via Vittorio Emanuele 17 - Stromboli
Tel. 090986118
Rates: double room in B&B, from 100 euros

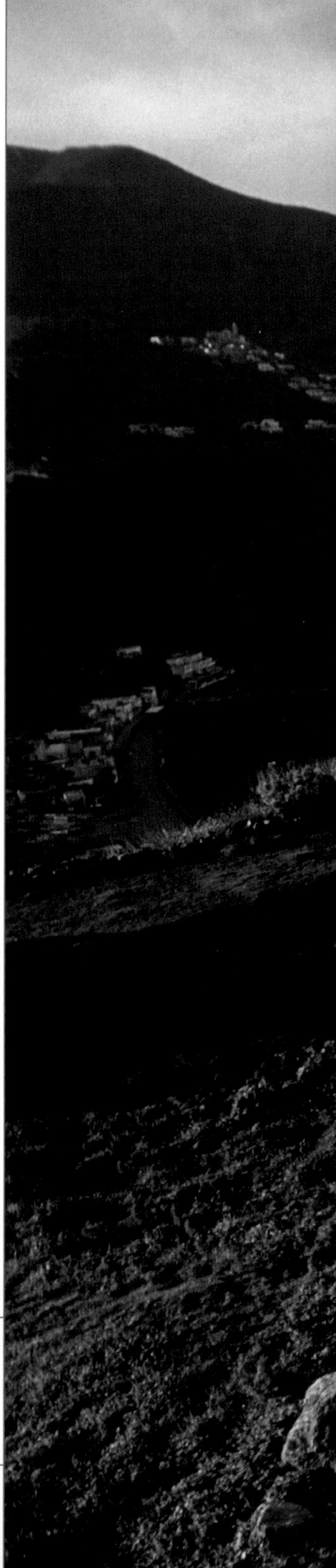

opened in the late 80s thanks to a careful restoration of the old Aeolian houses that used to keep the millstone and the olive-press on the inside. Nowadays, it offers 40 rooms in traditional Aeolian style, dipped into jasmines, bougainvilleas and vineyards, with a large terrace overlooking the sea of Malfa. If you walk for a few minutes and follow the path between houses, you can reach the stone beach of Punta Scario.
The wine resort Il Capo Faro opened in 2003 and is run by the Tasca d'Almerita family. It is a destination that attracts VIPs who take a trip around the islands. The wine company has been producing the delicious dessert wine Capo Faro on a five-hectare vineyard. For a day-trip out to the sea you can use the resort wooden pilot boat, the Pajarita, with eight comfortable seats to enjoy the lunch on board. By request, you can even go on a midnight squid fishing trip. There are few things that you have to experience in this island such as the caper festival organized in Malfa every year at the end of June and inaugurated by Slow Food, the popular Italian brand. Do not miss the Pollara city-tour, where you can buy capers directly from a factory and an evening out to see the sunset in Lingua. Make a stop to Alfredo's and enjoy his delicious crushed-ice drinks with seasonal fruits. The flavour of mulberries, figs, peaches and almonds still keeps an original and special taste. Do not miss the small ethno-anthropological museum, offering the true reconstruction of the ancient house of farmers who inhabited the islands. On the opposite side, you can see the little town of Rinella, with

Salina, take a rest in the terrace of the Capo Faro, on the right the prehistoric settlement of Capo Graziano in Filicudi

its small beach and its small port that you can admire from the terrace of the Ariana Hotel, where you can taste different local types of Malvasia wine. The tourists enjoy it especially out of season for its simple style and the proximity of the sea.

Alicudi and Filicudi, daughters of a minor god

Both of the islands, the closest to Sicily, are clearly visible from the Cefalù coasts; unlike the other islands, they have a quiet and autonomous life. Two volcanic cones on the sea with terraced vineyards, capers, olives, seasonal vegetables, dry-stone walls, a few nice white houses, goats, mules, donkeys, no cars, a small landing place and a few bars, restaurants and boarding houses as well as jagged coasts, rare beaches, unforgettable sunsets and a clear blue sea still teaming with fish. It is a paradise for the tourists who enjoy walking along paths of lava stones, going to the sea with local boats and enjoying the evening falling asleep under the stars. Situated on the western side of the archipelago, Alicudi, with fewer than 100 inhabitants, is characterized by its narrow streets that lead from the harbour to the centre where you can find a ho-

tel, a bar, a bazaar, a life lived in an ancient mountain village near the sea. The island was densely populated and it was involved in the Mediterranean obsidian trade as you can realize by visiting the first Bronze Age settlement and the pieces of pottery from the Roman age. It became more and more isolated because of some attacks from the sea and the frequent emigrations; for this reason today it offers a wonderful scenery in an uncontaminated nature.

The Fossa Felci Mountain dominates Filicudi. Its name derives from the Roman Phoenicusa that means rich in ferns; it offers different interesting areas such as Macine, the Neolithic village on the promontory above Capo Graziano and, in the same hill, the sacrificial area. At the harbour, in a small section at the Aeolian archaeological museum you can see events and battles that took place in the whole archipelago over the last millennium. After enjoying the local culinary delicacies such as the onion marmalade or the grouper fillets with

In the top on the left the small landing place of Alicudi, below a view of the hotel Signum of Salina.
In the top on the right, Capo Graziano in Filicudi, below the Canna rock

06

a green pepper sauce, do not miss the attractions on the Giafante and the Canna rocks situated a few miles away and the Bue Marino cave. It's worth a stop to the sea village Pecorini in order to admire the most suggestive sunsets where you can even find excellent the comfortable rooms at the boarding house La Sirena situated at a height of 6 metres above the sea level (Tel. 090988997, rates from 35 to 90 euros).

The Aegadian Islands out of season

The best magic moment to discover the Aegadian archipelago is in late spring, when it seems like the islands have just woke up after a very long sleep apparently lasted for centuries. They are rich in archaeological treasures, uncontaminated marine environments and ancient marine traditions. The island of Formica and the rock of Maraone are part of the Aegadian Islands.

Levanzo, whose ancient Roman name is Phorbantia, is a small paradise populated by two hundreds peopleth with a handful of small white houses around Cala Dogana, a small port that in summer attracts lots of scuba diving and seabed lovers.

The wonderful Marettimo is a real natural sanctuary with its ancient Hiera that sacred in Greece. It overlooks the crystal-clear sea of pizzo Falcone. Its seabed and caves are the most spectacular in the Mediterranean Sea and the Marine Reserve protects them. Marettimo is 600.000 years older than Levanzo and Favignana for its isolation and its geological history; from the naturalistic point of view it is one of the most interesting islands in Italy, a real rocky garden surrounded by the sea.

SPEND THE NIGHT AT THE EGADI

Marettimo Residence
Address: via Telegrafo, Marettimo
Tel. 0923923202
Rates: apartments from 52 euros per person

Paradiso
Address: via Lungomare 6, Levanzo
Tel. 0923924080
Rates: double room in half board from 140 euros

Residence L'Isola
Address: Levanzo
Tel. 3483904422
Rates: double room from 395 euros per week , package weekend 2 nights and 2 diving 200 euros

Hotel Aegusa
Addres: via Garibaldi 11, Favignana
Tel. 0923922430
Rates: double room in half board from 80 euros

Cave Bianche hotel
Address: municipal street Fanfalo - Favignana
Tel. 0923925451
Rates: B&B from 150 euros

Casa Favonio charming B&B
Address: contrada Seppi Torrente - Favignana
Tel. 0923 921179
Rates: B&B from 140 euros

On the left the small harbour of Levanzo, next to it a boat trip to the cave Cammello

A SITE YOU CANNOT MISS

Isola dei Conigli

From 1995, this island has been considered as an oriented natural reserve of Sicily. The bay can only be reached on foot or by swimming, it is secluded by the Protected Marine Area of the Pelagie Islands of the Ministry of the Environment. The site is protected for several reasons: the breathtaking beauty of the coastal and seaside landscape, the laying of the turtles' eggs sheltered by the young people of the WWF with periodical summer camps, but also the colony of seagulls nesting along the cliffs and the several vegetal endemism growing up among rocks and slopes. A difficult but exemplary intervention of reconstruction of the way down takes to the beach.

From March until July, before the busy landing of the tourists, it is possible to catch sight of regular dolphins, striped dolphins, bottle-nose dolphins, turtles, big carangidae, and if you are lucky, also the whale calves.

Four of them have been seen in the offing of Punta Grecale, in the A zone of the reserve.

There are more than 200 caves in this island and the local fishermen normally suggest to visit the most wonderful cave Cammello and Cattedrale. The sunken world of the Aegadian archipelago represents a true paradise for scuba divers. A luxuriant growth of posidonia sea plant covers its seabed that represents a precious habitat for fish species production and, between Favignana and Levanzo, it creates a continuous and intact cover that has an extraordinary value.

At Favignana, the first two tuna fishing nets of San Leonardo and San Nicolò were probably erected under the Arabs and subsequently under the Angevin domination. The tuna fishing net of San Cusumano is the only one all over Italy. The islands belonged to the Pallavicini Rusconi family of Genoa until 1874 and then they were bought by the powerful Florio family, a great dynasty of entrepreneurs who built a small economic empire of the sea around the big fishing net. Recently, after a long and complicated renovation, the Florio building is finally open to the public with a museum, an exhibition area and some guest rooms. You can assist to the tuna slaughter, guided by the rais, which takes place in May. The fishermen, (nearly 50 of them are members of a cooperative), do not throw encircling nets into the sea every year instead the fish go towards the death chamber. Looking at the slaughter rite is becoming more and more difficult; you can see big black boats, placed squarely, and exhausted fishermen who sing the "cialomè", a typical Arabian song, when they pull up their nets with harpooned fish surrounded by foam and blood.

Favignana with its typical tuff quarries, on the right the natural reserve of the Isola dei Conigli in Lampedusa, protected area for the reproduction of turtles

Lampedusa, boats and resorts

The name of the Pelagie archipelago comes from the Greek Pelaghié that means high sea islands. Lampedusa is the flattest and the most calcareous and volcanic island with green vegetable plots and gardens. Linosa and Lampione are located quite in the middle of the Sicilian channel. At the beginning of the season going on holidays to Lampedusa can be very quiet, enjoying boat day trips and beaches that are still empty. At the most elegant resorts, except for July and August, the prices are accessible. The Gattopardo Club and The Calandra, at Cala Creta, are the best places all over the island: fourteen "dammusi" (dialect word that means roof) with a private terrace dipped into a stone garden overlooking the silent cliff rising steeply from the north-facing bay with a private slope to reach the rocky beach. Sea lovers have the chance to use every day two comfortable wooden fishing boats, the Tatami and the Balù, having lunch on board with traditional local dishes: aubergines and peppers stew, meatballs with tomato sauce, marinated shrimps and mullets, small vegetable omelettes and fruits as much as you like. At the Calandra, there is a "younger" atmosphere: background music in a cactus garden enlightened by the sunset and a local happy hour. There are other ways to explore the island on the boat in one week: there is the Rosa dei Venti, the Cala Madonna, the Medusa, and also comfortable boarding houses at the sea such as the Cavalluccio Marino with special fish dishes; and for those who go on holiday with children we recommend the Costa House, a holiday farm with poultry.

SPEND THE NIGHT IN LAMPEDUSA

Gattopardo di Lampedusa
Address: via Cala Creta
Tel. 0922970883
Equinoxe: 011885211
Rates: one week, full board, car and boat from 1220 euros

La Calandra Club
Address: Lampedusa - Contrada Cala Creta
Tel. 0922971098 / 3356166005
Equinoxe: 0118185211
Kids: from 14 years old
Rates: half board, boat and scooter from 1260 euros

La Medusa
Address: Piazza Medusa 3
Tel. 0922970126,
Rates: half board 80-180 euros per day, per person

Cupola Bianca
Address: via Contrada Madonna
Tel. 0922971274 / 0922975793
Rates: half board 110-170 euros per day, per person

U Piddu
Address: via Madonna 10
Tel. 0922971050
Rates: 730-1360 euros per week, half board, a boat and 5 meals, kids from 12 years old

Cala Madonna Club
Address: contrada Madonna 28
Tel. 0922971626
Rates: 175-225 euros per day full board

Linosa, the last paradise

It is the last forgotten paradise of the Sicilian sea. Unlike Lampedusa, nearly one hour far from it by hydrofoil, this island does not have valuable hotels. You can find a residence and a holiday house with a dozen of rooms. Those who want to relax by enjoying the sea on the dream seabed and natural views can rent a room. Simple white and colourful cubes in the middle of the country full of gardens and irrigated vegetable plots. Water cannot run out thanks to the desalter. Capers and prickly pears, vineyards and well-groomed fruit gardens grow among the dry walls of the black lava, on basins situated between the three extinct volcanic cones that form the inner part of Linosa. Except for the week of August 15th, the island is considered a paradise by the scuba diving lovers attracted by the Secchitella groupers, which is one of the most ten suggestive dive sites of the Mediterranean Sea. If you are not a seabed explorer, you can enjoy your long and quite days at the sea in one of the northeast marine coasts that you can reach following comfortable dirt path leading to the rocks and forming huge natural pools perfect for a good swim. From the district Mannarazza to the lighthouse, from the natural pool to the stacks, in some places you can even enjoy a good rest in the small squares. The fishermen of the island are descendents of the Spanish families who repopulated Linosa under the Bourbon domination and some of them organize boat day trips, late evening fishing, or a visit to the spectacular colonies of Berta Maggiore in the offing of Mannarazza.

The local cuisine offers a taste of ancient flavours of the sea and the land. There are two popular restaurants: Da Anna (Tel. 0922972048), specialized in cooking lentil soups and couscous with groupers. It also offers a covered veranda out of the country where you can taste pizzas or schiacciata (flat oven-baked Italian bread). At the Scalo Vecchio overlooking the fishing boats in the harbour, Caterina Errera cooks a variety of very tasty vegetable starters, spaghetti with homemade in-oil tuna and small delicious local capers (Tel. 0922972941). In the rest of the evening you can enjoy other island bars, at the Scalo Vecchio or along the main street, taste crushed-ice drinks made with seasonal fruit, especially the one made with prickly pears, eat a fig or almond dessert, listen to live guitar and drink a glass of cold Zibibbo wine. There is just one pub open until very late at night on the turtle's beach, the Black Planet, where you can admire another sunset among the purple, red and yellow volcanic tuff rocks and listen to the music under the stars.

Linosa, volcanic rocks in the natural pools

Pantelleria, a stay in a "dammuso"

August is the best time to visit it. You can get to the island by plane or by boat. The island is huge and the coast is indented so, it doesn't seems to be so busy as it is. There are just few beaches, for this reason it is better to go for a day trip by boat; you can rent one at the harbour. In the island you can breathe the African air that also evokes the African colours. You can sleep in a fresh dammuso or in a resort hidden among the rocks. One of the most beautiful beaches is the Elefante where you can admire the cove of Cala Tramontana. In Pantelleria, the dammusi with white dome-like roofs, the volcanic dry stonewalls, the slow-growing trees, carefully cultivated and the aligned vineyards create a perfect geometric shape between the sky and the sea. At the opposite side, you can admire the enlightened Sicilian coast. As a matter of fact, Pantelleria is further south than Tunis. It is a beautiful island, even out of season, for its spectacular lake of Venus with its therapeutic mud and hot waters. In autumn, you can visit the cellars, most of them open in the afternoon, where you can enjoy the local Passito wine. Do not miss a walk through the archaeological sites in the district of Mursia and in the city centre. The Cala Levante and the Cala Gadir seabed are two wonderful dive sites, appreciated for their submerged archaeological wrecks. If you want to spend the night plunged in a particular atmosphere and you are not interested in renting a dammuso, you can choose the Dream Resort, opened few years ago, with a small wellness centre. It has 40 typical local style suites situated halfway up the hill plunged in the green of a Mediterranean garden. The Zubebi Resort (Tel. 0923913653) is situated above the city centre among the hills and is famous for the Zibibbo wine production where you can enjoy an ethnic and a very relaxing atmosphere. ■

Pantelleria, the typical architecture and the Church of St. Vincenzo, below some vineyards and terraces of the island

Levanzo, the archaeological underwater site of Cala Minnola

07 EXPLORING THE SEABED

LOOKING FOR UNDERWATER TREASURES

Under the Sicilian sea there is a hidden museums. The Marine Superintendency has recently carried out scuba divers itineraries that by passing through some of the minor islands, with the help of qualified guides, will enable you to discover Hellenistic, Roman and medieval finds situated in their original places

Aeolian Islands: Panarea and Filicudi

Scenery of incomparable marine beauty and of renowned archaeological interest is the ring of reefs in front of the small Panarea formed by Basiluzzo, Lisca Bianca, Spinazzola, Formiche and Panarelli.

On the crags of the islet Basiluzzo you can find the remains of an imperial Roman residence. There, the itinerary "Strutture di Basiluzzo" is marked; it winds down from 5 to 12 metres of depth among the remains of a quay that sank afterwards. However, from the last remarks, the archaeologists think that it could have been a fishpond, a masonry system made of huge rocky blocks that used to improve the fish farming. The diving is extremely simple and can be done together with a skilled guide of the Amphibia diving (Tel. 3351245332); you only have to follow the white cord plunged among the rocks and fractures rich in madrepore and coloured encrustments.

For a watchful sub, surprising is the phenomenon of the gassy fumaroles characterized by the bubbles, typical of the seabed of Panarea. The diving in Basiluzzo is an occasion to sail around the entire islet covered by the wonderful Mediterranean vegetation

A MUSEUM YOU CANNOT MISS

The Bernabò Brea Museum

Dedicated to the archaeologist that used to dig the island since the 50s, the museum is included in the medieval castle of Lipari.

On the inside, you can go over the phases of the Aeolian history: prehistory, classical age, the epigraphic pavilion and volcanology. They are the only vestiges of the Greek-Roman period, together with the theatre masks of the 3rd century BC.

Address: via del Castello - Lipari

Tel. 0909880174

Opening: Mon to Sat 9 to 1.30 p.m. and 3 to 7 p.m.

Sun from 9 to 1.30 p.m.

In the top on the left, a panoramic view of Lipari and its castle.
Here, an old mask of the museum Bernabò Brea.
Above, the seabed of Basiluzzo in Panarea with the gaseous fumaroles

such as the rare dwarf palm and plunge into the amazing natural pools near Lisca Bianca. This is an unusual way to discover the secret naturalistic beauty of this small volcanic pearl of the Aeolian Islands, rich in history since the first life forms in the Mediterranean as the settlements of Capo Milazzese proves. If you want to spend the night, besides the very popular hotel Raya, you can go to the small resort and great restaurant Da Pina Mandarano (Tel. 090983324).

In the blue sea of Filicudi, in Punta Graziano, the scuba divers having a second level licence, can dive down to 45 metres of depth, together with local qualified guides, with the diving centre I Delfini (Tel. 3401484645), in order to admire the remains of the wreck A of the 2nd century BC and the cable-laying ship "Città di Milano" sank to the bottom in 1919.

Some scuba divers in the seabed of Marettimo, on the right, a detail of the asteroids, below, the cave Cammello

Aegadi: Levanzo

The island is all there, placed around the small harbour of Cala Dogana, a crib of white houses and blue windows all gathered around the beach of sand with a sea that looks like a mirror.

The seabed of Levanzo is considered as the most important archaeological site of the Mediterranean belonging to a Punic-Roman era.

If you want to visit the wreck of Cala Minnola, call the guard of the place Chiara Marraffa (Tel. 3895152632) that, on require, will put the equipment for the diving at your disposal. There, 80 Roman amphorae, more or less undamaged, lie at 25 metres of depth. They belonged to a big cargo ship that ran aground. Visit the Marine Superintendency website (www.regione.sicilia.it/beniculturali/ sopmare).

The second diving you cannot miss is Capo Grosso in the northeastern coast of the island. It offers the same exciting view: several metal amphorae now corroded by the seaweeds, they are in line on the crystal seabed among octopuses, white sea breams and wonderful sponges and belong to the Roman fleet that in those waters fought the Phoenicians in the historical battle of the Aegadian Islands. Also interesting is the excursion by land of the Genovese cave with its rock painting (Tel. 0923924032).

Marettimo

At Cala Spalmatore, on a 12 metres seabed, you can find different iron guns untidily scattered on the sandy and rocky bottom, and several shells. It is almost sure that they belonged to a pirate ship that, as usual, used to take shelter near the hidden Cala Spalmatore where it was possible to run aground the ships and where there was fresh water. For the pirates coming from the north of Africa, it was the perfect place to hide before or after the raid in the Sicilian land. Even if it is a reserve, you can visit this place with one of the guides of Vito Torrente (Tel. 3333772866).

Marettimo offers at least 25 scuba divings for more or less skilled divers. You can ask Fabio Tedone of the Marettimo Diving Center (Tel. 0923921302). The island is really extraordinary for the crystal clarity of the water, for its colours but also for the flora and the fauna. You can admire from the gorgonians that cover the narrow gorges, the rocks and canyons at 20 metres of depth, the fake coral, the huge sponges, the coloured walls of astroides, to the spectacular oceanic Neptune Grass. Start with the simplest diving like the rock of the Cammello and the Orlo di San Simone at the old harbour in order to try your ability and trim and then you could try the more difficult ones, such as Punta Bassana, with its variety of seabed among narrow gorges and hiding places full of fish like groupers, moray eels and big white sea breams. However, the unforgettable experience in Marettimo is the diving in the cave. You cannot miss the Camino, the Tuono cave and the Cattedrale.

Pelagie: Linosa

Situated at 400 metres from the east coast in the C zone of the protected area of the Pelagie Islands, the Secchitella is a 200 metres long submerged ridge that goes from north to south. The Cappello della Secca, in the northern part, is at less than 3.5 metres of depth and its length is divided by a 10 metres canyon that is 30 metres deep. It has a sharp and pointed ridge that separates both the slopes. It is considered as the most beautiful diving of the entire archipelago, and the best in Italy for the transparency of the water. Here, you can experience 7 to 8 different scuba divings, in short a whole holiday. You can start with two exploratory divings at 30 metres of depth in order

The rocks of Linosa,
on the right Ustica, a diving
in the rocks of the Medico

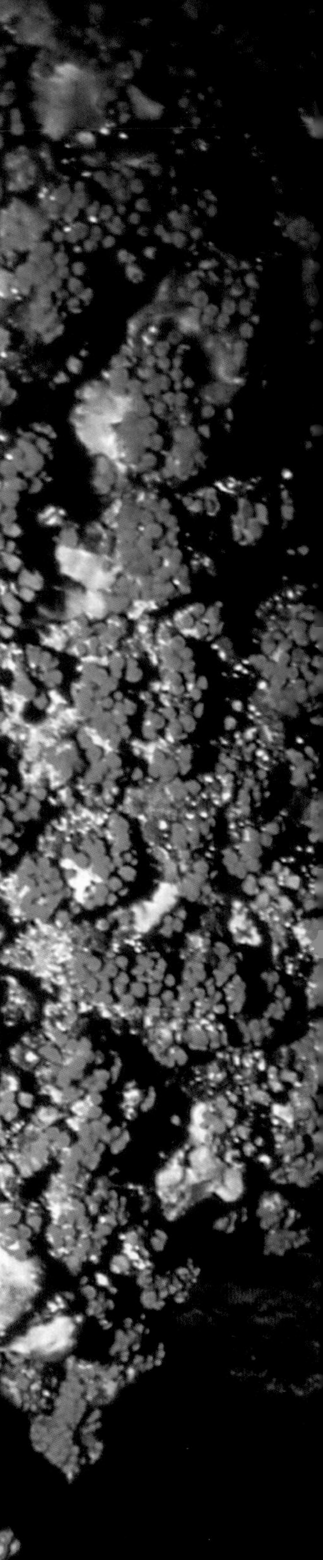

to understand the geography of the shoal. Except for the gorgonian, here you can see lots of things starting from the spectacular wall entirely covered with orange madrepore (astroides calycularis). You can also see a big quantity of fish such as the grouper, the white and black sea bream, the dentex, the amberjack, the barracuda and the carangid.
Another diving: at 40 metres of depth you can see the deepest part of the wall, the cave of the shrimps, the den of the big groupers and the archaeological finds.
The archaeological route includes 11 finds made of stone and lead anchor stocks and old remains of amphorae (Linosa Diving Center, Tel. 0922972054, Mare Nostrum Tel. 0922972042).

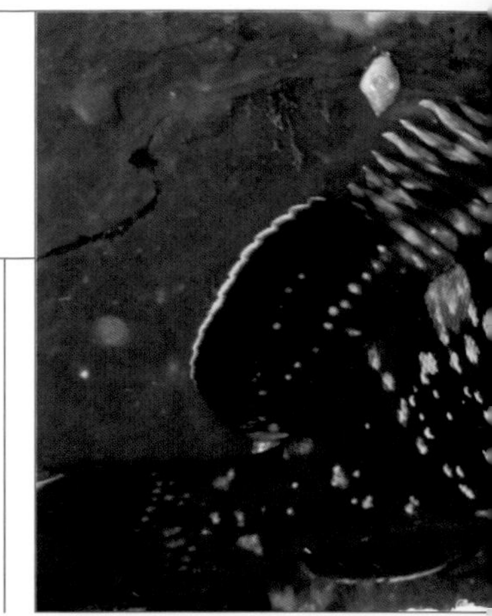

Pantelleria, a grouper and below the dawn on the Arco dell'Elefante

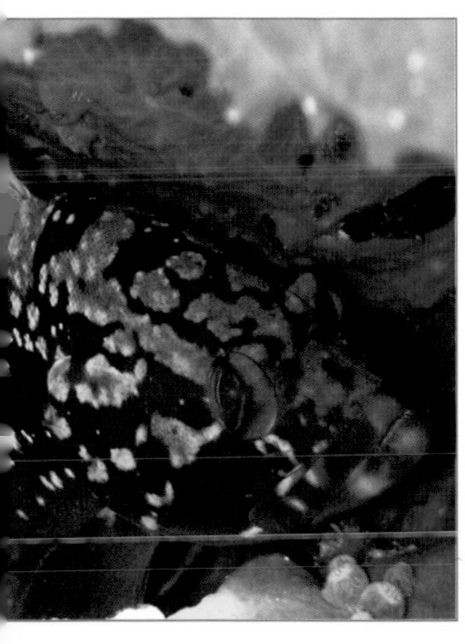

Pantelleria

Last European strip of volcanic origin, it is a naturalistic heaven where the landscape bewitches the tourist looking for strong emotions. The diving at the Punic Archeosub site, on the seabed of the Gadir bay, is of middling difficulty, suitable for those who have a I or II level licence. You can start by leaving from the landing place of Gadir with the guides of the Dive X of Eddi Famularo, (Tel. 0923915594). After 15 metres you can already see the first shards of amphorae among the sand, the Neptune grass and the rocks full of sea anemones, or narrow gorges where groupers and moray eels hide. Go on until 25-30 metres of depth and look at the other undamaged lean anchors two metres long. It is very interesting for the several finds, especially for the Punic anchors that probably belonged to two different wrecks that date back to the end of the 3rd century and the first half of the 2nd century BC. The itinerary of Gadir proves that Pantelleria was one of the main ports of call both in the Carthaginian and in the Roman age.

A wreckage on the seabed of Ustica, on the right an alley that leads to the harbour, below a Bourbon cannon

Ustica: the divers' heaven

It only takes one hour to reach the island by hydrofoil from the harbour of Palermo, or two hours if you go by ship. There are few and small guesthouses around the square of the fishermen's village standing on the harbour, few small restaurants where you can eat fresh fish and a couple of restaurant for divers and boatmen where the booking is necessary especially in high season. Clean and warm are the rooms for rent in the alleys. In the morning, at the front door, you can find people selling fresh vegetables picked in the backyard, and organic food having a special taste and smell: tomatoes, courgettes, vegetables, lentils from Ustica, prickly pear preserves, apricots and mulberries. Also good is the local white wine Albanella.There is only one big hotel, the Grotta Azzurra, built in the 60s,

but still under restoration; a good and new one is the hotel Clelia (0918449039) and the sea-view residence Stella Marina (091 8448121) If you want to go diving, contact the Alta Marea with a big and comfortable boat (Tel. 3381850289).

The Ustica Marine Protected Area, blue flag of the European Union for clean sea, is one of the most important area of the Italian coast, suggested in the blue guide of Legambiente. The Marine Reserve has protected Ustica sea, has reduced the motor boats, the fishing and the presence of bathers in a great part of the seabed and the coasts. The several diving centres offer diving classes in 15 sites; they are all qualified and situated around the island. If you want to go diving on the archaeological sites call the Diving Orca Sub (Tel. 3388882236).

If you want to go diving on the archaeological sites call the Diving Orca Sub (Tel. 3388882236). ■

Sciacca, a panoramic view of the harbour

08

SMALL VILLAGES
HOLIDAY AND GASTRONOMY

Spend your holiday with the fishermen of the seaside small villages of the western Sicily in order to go fishing and refind the old flavours of the sea. Do not forget to explore the innerland and to spend your time in the new countryside resorts

The island is full of small villages. Sheltered by the city or in the small islands, there are so many villages that no one has ever taken the trouble to count them.

Spending your holiday in a village also means putting out to sea for the traditional fishing and rediscovering the local gastronomy or the nouvelle cuisine, the Arabian influence and old recipes that here always taste like earth and sea.

In the morning, the fresh fish becomes a real show: it is placed on the market stalls of the big marines of the island in the harbours of Mazara del Vallo and Sciacca where you can find the richest fishing boats of Sicily going towards the Channel and Africa. From here, not all the catch flies on the way to the markets of the northern Italy. Some of it is used to fill with pleasure the small and big restaurants of the coastal area. Sicily is considered the home of wine, olive oil and fish. Actually, thanks to the Arabian influence, from Trapani to Agrigento, Sicily becomes a really charming place and offers tasty works of genius such as the fish and vegetable couscous, the almond caponata and plenty of dessert wines renowned all over the world.

Once you leave Palermo, beyond the lines of the Isolotto delle Femmine with its very small fishing harbour, make a stop at the small vil-

A restaurant of the beach of Portopalo, Menfi, some fishermen working at the sea-coast of Castellammare del Golfo, below the Spanish Tower of Menfi

lage of Terrasini. Situated between the coast and the mountain, surrounded by a beach blocked by the stacks lighted at night, Terrasini is full of white little houses and a square dominated by the church. Here, the mass tourism seems not to be a problem for the life and the pace of the fishermen. Get near the harbour and you will see, one next to the other, the several small restaurants on the promenade around Palazzo D'Aumale, a 19th-century residence where the prince Henry, related to the king of France, used to keep the wines produced in his estate. Nowadays, the building has turned into a modern historic-anthropological museum with interesting scientific departments. It also keeps an amazing collection of Sicilian carts, miniature models of old boats and a collection of shells and fossils. Very impressive is the local cooking with its ethnic and spicy touch made of seasonal fish, prawns and tuna fish. You can try all this at the restaurant Prima Fila (Tel. 0918684422) on the beautiful panoramic terrace next to the small church overlooking the harbour.
Before you get to Trapani, visit another historic small village, Castellammare del Golfo, in Arabic Al Madarig. It is one of the oldest fishing fleets of the island open to the tourism. On the mooring quay it is easy to rent a boat or a rubber dinghy in order to visit the wonderful coves. Very impressive is Cala Marina, the promenade near the harbour dominated by

AT THE **THERMAL BATHS** SCIACCA AND ACQUAPIA

Next to the old spring, inside a green equipped park you can find the spa "Acqua Pia" where the pure hot water pours and nourishes the thermal spring. It has been recently built and has comfortable rooms and a big park.
The spa is at the boundaries between Palermo, Agrigento and Trapani in the heart of the Western Sicily in the district of Montevago at an altitude of 56 metres.
There are two thermal pools, one for adults and one for children. They have beneficial springs pouring the thermal water at 40°C and an unusual sitting room inside the old "basin of the women" where it is possible to emulate the Roman rites.
The spa occupies a big terrace on the Sicilian channel; it overlooks the old harbour, the boats, vineyards and beaches from the right to the left. In the rooms below, the beauty treatments are carried out among mud baths, steam, clay and sulphurous vapours.
You can buy wellness, restyling and relax-tourism packages.
Few kilometres later, on the mount Kronio that dominates the city, you can find the steam vent of San Calogero, very old natural hot caves.
You will feel like you descend into the underworld and then go back to earth (Tel. 0925961111).

08

The Porto Canale of Mazara del Vallo, on the top the sunset on the harbour of Sciacca

the Aragonese castle that hosts a small maritime museum.

In the storehouses and in the spaces of the old tunny-fishing area, a new modern hotel stands, the Cetarium Hotel, 26 rooms, the most beautiful are on the first floor and have a view on the seashore. It also has a restaurant inside a vaulting room and an open-air bar under a lighted palm where you can lay on the pillows of the comfortable ottoman. Not far from the harbour, in a big residence with a garden, placed among the houses, you can find the new three stars hotel Cerri. It is functional and modern and has small suites overlooking the sea. If you want to experience the emotion of the fresh fish, get up early in the morning and wait for the fishing boats to arrive; the fish is immediately unloaded and put up for auction with gestures and languages that a layman cannot understand.

From Mazara del Vallo to Sciacca

In the Porto Canale of Mazara, you can find one of the biggest fleets of the Mediterranean. The deep-sea fishing consists of 350 big fishing bo-

ats that stay in the sea for several weeks; there are also about a hundred fishing boats for the unprofessional fishing. Under the turn of the Porto Canale, the market of the retailing fish is a real show that recurs every day from 7 to 10 a.m. except for Sunday. In front of it, in an old coal establishment, now restored, you can find the restaurant-fish shop of the Marmomio family, fishermen for generations. People usually go to the fish shop in order to buy the tuna fish; latest news is the tuna fish jelly and the botargo, the one with the dark veins. You can also buy delicious appetizers or fried fish having a memorable taste. Also impressive is the small and red local lobster. A genuine flavour of the sea can be found in the typical cooking of the Bettola (Tel. 09323946422); the restaurant doesn't have an open-air terrace, but the fish couscous is excellent as well as the wide range of vegetables and fish appetizers.
If you want to buy authentic Tunisian carpets, few steps from the harbour, there is the cooperative Amal run by local and Tunisian craftswomen. The overhand knot carpets are worked with a handloom on an unrefined ground, and show the geometrical figures typical of the Berber brooch. The cooperative also sells white and blue ceramic saucepans.
Drive back towards the hills, get past the archaeological area of Selinunte

GOLF AND WELLNESS
VERDURA RESORT

The Golf Resort has just opened; it is on the sea of Sciacca and is called Rocco Forte. The building stretches over an area of 250 hectares, 120 hectares are used for two golf courses, one has 18 holes and the other only 9.
There are 200 rooms in a complex of villas next to a wellness centre with 16 rooms. It is 30 kilometres away from Agrigento, near Sciacca.
Address: district Verdura Sciacca (AG)
Rates: standard single rooms from 400 euros

PLACES YOU CANNOT MISS

Sea flavours and B&Bs

In one side there is capo S. Marco, in the other side the small fishermen's village Porto Palo di Menfi. The sea is cold and clean, full of shells and dunes, rich in African vegetation and the blinding sun shines over it; it has been a European blue flag for years. Vittorio, the chef from Bergamo, has his origins and fulfils his dreams here.

On the terrace there are 40 tables all set under an arcade lighted with candles and spotlights. Here, you can taste the delicacies of the Sicilian sea still luxuriant as well as the Sicilian land. The lazy people could idle about on the beach sitting on deck-chairs with beach umbrellas right under the terrace of the restaurant that now is also a B&B; they could take a shower and then have dinner. The first courses are made of prawns, paddlefish and lobsters, the specialty is the fish soup made with grouper, teleost fish, pheasant fish, scorpion fish, and delicacies from the vegetable garden. Try the triumphal salad full of shellfish. Among the main courses, the best one is the saffron-flavoured risotto with mussels, or the spaghetti with the lobster. Very good is the thinly sliced octopus or shrimp, and finally the fruit of the surrounding gardens: the Malvasia-flavoured cantaloupe, apricots, medlars and from June also the first figs. Excellent is the wine list, almost all Sicilian wines, recommended by the chef.

Da Vittorio
Address: Porto Palo di Menfi, via Friuli Venezia Giulia 9 (AG)
Tel. 092578381

and the natural reserve of the river Belice, and you will find Menfi, the city of the wine with its renowned cellars Planeta (for guided tours Tel. 0916124335). The hill landscape shows rows of tidy vineyards as far as the eye can see; they stretch towards the wide beaches of Portopalo and Fiori, white-golden sand, surrounded by the Mediterranean vegetation that grows on the dunes.

If you want to spend the night, go to the new opening Foresteria di casa Planeta (district Passo di Gurra, Menfi, highway 115, tel. 09251955460). There are 14 rooms, all have different colours and antique pieces of furniture with an ethnic taste; it is a modern building surrounded by vineyards and sea, but also by a pool and an unusual garden created like it was a nursery. To the Foresteria, in the countryside of Menfi, in the province of Agrigento, you will feel like you were plunged into the nature and the Mediterranean peace, among the dwarf palms, gardens of cactus, citrus orchards, and a dozen of variety of rosemary, thyme, lavender and lentisk.

Let's now move from the wine to the sea. The fishing boat Margherita, goes from Portopalo di Menfi to Sciacca and Mazara del Vallo following the orders of Margherita Di

A dish with shrimps at Vittorio's, on the right a detail of the garden of Kolymbetra in Agrigento

SPEND THE NIGHT IN THE SMALL VILLAGES

Hotel Cetarium
Address: Cala Marina
Castellammare del Golfo (TP)
Tel. 0924533401
Rates: double room from 120 euros

Cerri Hotel
Address: via Mascagni 2
Castellammare del Golfo (TP)
Tel. 092434999
Rates: double room from 80 to 115 euros

Castello di Falconara Resort
Address: Marina di Butera, (CL)
Tel. 0583081081
Rates: double room from 189 euros

Mandranova
Address: Palma di Montechiaro, district Mandranova (AG)
Tel: 0916120463 - 3939862169
Rates: double room from 110 to 140 euros, suite from 130 to 250 euros (lunch on the boat from 400 euros for 6 people)

Baglio della Luna Hotel and Restaurant
Address: district Maddalusa, (AG)
Tel. 0922511061
Rates: double room from 200 euros

Feola, a woman that has the licence to bring the tourists fishing for an entire weekend, all year long. The boat is very comfortable and well equipped for overnight stays. If you want to spend the night and eat in the countryside, by the fresh air of the vineyards, call the restaurant Il Vigneto (Tel. 092571732) situated in a cottage with a wonderful Mediterranean garden. You will find not only fish but also first courses of the local cooking made with fennel and ricotta cheese. Try the "pasta'ncaciatà" made with veal ragout, almonds and cloves. In Menfi, you can spend the night in the countryside and enjoy the comforts of the holiday farm Tenuta Stoccatello, 5 kilometres from the sea. It also offers relaxing and treatments as well as a small swimming pool (Tel. 3339035428).
In Sciacca, enjoy the view of the harbour with the old city that dominates it, and try the excellent gastronomy on the terrace of the restaurant Porto San Paolo (Tel. 092527982), with its tables ranged against the quay. Triumphal are the spaghetti with the lobster. In the morning, it is not difficult to watch the typical auction of the fresh fish and listen to the shouting of the fishermen. If you want to spend the night in a very special atmosphere, drive 20 kilometres more towards the beach and the castle of Falconara after the built-up area of Agrigento.

Here, the terrace of the resort Mandranova, in the opposite page the yard of the farm Mosè

The seafood, from Licata to Palma di Montechiaro

The Falconara Charming House Resort standing around the castle on the beach belongs to the family Bordonaro. It has sixty-four rooms, half of them in the clubhouse with large suite-apartments, and other twelve near the farm. It has a terrace overlooking the garden or the beach and 10 valuable suites, each one having the name of the several nobles that used to own the castle.

For an unforgettable gastronomic stopover, according to the suggestions of the best food-and-wine guidebooks, do not miss the sophisticated cooking of the Madia in Licata (Tel. 0922771443). Few tables, only by reservation, it offers a sophisticated version of the traditional seafood recipes.

The wide beaches, popular just for the inhabitants of Licata, stand on the right of the new quay dominated by the Norman fort. They are the shore of Marianello, dominated by wonderful gullies and, further on, the beach Torre di Gaffe surrounded by the rocks of Punta Bianca. If you want to go fishing, try the Montecristo, a wooden double-mast built in 1939, anchored in the quay.

Leave the coast and make a stopover in the hinterland. It is not just the classic trip out of Agrigento (only 27 kilometres away), it is in-

A PLACE YOU CANNOT MISS

The Kolymbetra garden

D The atmosphere that wraps up all the people that plunge in the silence of the Kolymbetra garden is really special. 5 hectares of citrus fruits, olive trees and rare plants growing around the Temple of Dioscuri and the Temple of Vulcano in the core of the Valle dei Templi of Agrigento. Today, the FAI (Italian National Trust) runs it. After a long restoration, with the past of the years, the area was used as an orchard, it was an unexpected Eden, where the Mediterranean scrub alternates with mulberry, carob, prickly pear, almond and huge Saracen olive trees. It is a real shelter from the summer heat and a perfect place for meditation. Kolymbetra inspired the novel "I vecchi e i giovani" by Pirandello that was born in the near district Caos. The nearest Porto Empedocle, for many people is simply Vigàta; it is the village of Montalbano (the most famous character of the novels by Andrea Camilleri), which is a genuine "empedoclino" (inhabitant of Porto Empedocle).

SPEND THE NIGHT

Villa Romana

Four stars hotel, it has about 40 rooms with sea view, a pool and an equipped beach.

Address: promenade Nettuno Porto Empedocle (AG)

Tel. 092263417

Rates: double room 150 euros

Fattoria Mosè

Apartments for rent surrounded by ancient olive trees (for 2-6 people).

Address: via M. Pascal 4 (AG)

Tel. 0922606115,

Rates: B&B from 48 euros

08

The fleet of Sciacca, on the right the temple of the Concordia framed by some blossom almond trees

FISHING TIME

Portopalo di Menfi Il Veliero
Tel. 3407726997
Rates: 35 euros

Pescaturismo Margherita
Tel. 3333813477 - 3203467675
Rates: 55-65 euros per person, lunch included

Licata Stella Maris
Tel. 3332813076
Bialberi Montecristo
by Gaetano Ripellino
fishing night for at least 11 people
Rates: 80 euros per person

stead a walk in search of the real origins of the writer of The Leopard novel, Giuseppe Tomasi di Lampedusa. As a matter of fact, here in Palma di Montecristo, founded in 1637 by the duke Carlo Tomasi, prince of Lampedusa, everything unravels around the noble family. The foundation stone was laid in order to build the chapel of the ducal palace that was turned into a Convent of the Benedictine nuns. The village, having an octagonal plan, stands on a rocky hill and dominates the valley that stretches down to the sea. The most important monuments are the ducal palace, the beautiful Mother Church, the Tower of San Carlo, S. Maria della Luce and the castle of Montechiaro built by the Chiaramonte family and situated in a strategic position above the sea.
Palma has always been a destination for gastronomic pilgrimages linked to the art of cooking of the enclosed nuns of the Monastery and a couple of historic laboratories that make sweets, biscuits and the marzipan paschal lamb seasoned with every kind of delicacy. ■

AGRIGENTO

A MUSEUM YOU CANNOT MISS

Archaeological Museum of Agrigento

Showcase of the history of Valle dei Templi (valley of the temples), the museum was founded from the fusion of the new museum structure and the restored bodies of the 14th-century convent of San Nicola, former agora of the old city where the library, the conference room and the auditorium stand. From the prehistory and the Hellenization phase, following both a chronological and a topographic order, there are 15 rooms describing the extraordinary history of the people that used to live there. It represents a big example of art and civilization. Among the most valuable works of art, there is the renowned Efebo of Agrigento of the 480 BC; it is in the 10th room, as well as the charming reconstruction of the telamon coming from the temple of Zeus Olympus in the 6th room.

Opening: From 9 a.m. to 1 p.m.
Tel. 0922552611

It is one of the most popular destinations of the island. Pindaro, described its inhabitants in this way "They build their monuments like if they have to live for ever, and have fun like if they have to die tomorrow". There is an itinerary in the old town of Agrigento able to combine culture and food-and-wine. It consists in six stops from piazza Don Minzoni, the higher part of the so-called hill of San Geraldo, until via Atenea, the core of the city full of historic buildings, churches, shops and bars. This itinerary is called "spizziculiata" (bit by bit) because you can admire the monumental and cultural part of Agrigento, but also peck at local products along a path that offers from the appetizer to the dessert. Several associations working with tourists have examined the itinerary; actually they are able to describe the spirit of the city going through the history and the several theatres, of course Pirandello is ahead of everybody.

The starting point is piazza Don Minzoni where the Cathedral stands. It is dedicated to Saint Gerland, bishop of the re-evangelization of the beginning of the second millennium; it was widened over the centuries until the baroque period. Go on towards the several streets and alleys until you get to the Church of Santa Maria dei Greci, the first Cathedral of Agrigento, built at the end of the first millennium on the remains of a Doric temple offered to Athena. It is still possible to see some parts of the podium and some columns. From here, always walking, enter in a maze of alleys until you get to the monumental complex Santo Spirito where still today there is a convent for enclosed Benedictine Cistercian nuns. Finally, get to via Atenea, hearth of the city rich in fashion, art and product showcases.

Along the itinerary you will find a range of shops and new inns available for all the tourists that want to taste the pane "cunzato" (filled) with olives and oil, the pasta with anchovies cooked at the Agrigento way, the wine, the meat nibbles and also the almond, pistachio and candied pumpkin desserts prepared by the nuns of the Spirito Santo with some recipes handed down over the centuries. Those same ingredients are also used for the sweet couscous, exclusive specialty of Agrigento.

If you want to spend the night eating sushi and drinking excellent Sicilian and foreign wines, go to the Fouquet's Bar at the Mosé village. ■

The entrance of the cathedral in the old town centre, on the right the Temple of Juno

A SITE YOU CANNOT MISS

The archaeological area

It is divided into an east zone (Temple of Hercules, Concordia, Juno, Tomb of Theron) and a west zone (Temple of Jupiter, Dioscuri, Esculapium, Sanctuary of Demeter and Kore) by the highway 118. In both sides there is a parking area, the ticket office, information on guided tours.

Tel. 0922621611
Opening: 8,30 a.m. -7/8 p.m. in summer
Ticket: 8 euros
The 10 euros ticket includes the entrance at the Archaeological Museum

SPEND THE NIGHT IN AGRIGENTO

Villa Athena Hotel

It is the only hotel of the archaeological area that overlooks the temples. There, you can fall asleep looking at them and dreaming about the history.

Address: via Ugo La Malfa 3
Tel. 0922596288
Rates: from 130 to 210 euros

Atenea 191 B&B

18th-century building, it was restored with few, elegant rooms in the city centre. It has frescoed terraces overlooking the temples.

Address: via Atenea 191
Tel. 0922595594
Rates: from 65 euros

Taormina, S. Domenico hotel

09

TAORMINA
UNDER THE VOLCANO

Take a trip in the environs of the Sicilian's tourism capital. The small town in the province of Messina is loved by the foreign tourists for its traditions and events that attract international music, cinema, and theatre stars, but also for the big hotels for VIPs and the restored villa resorts. Taormina, always gives the best of it

Taormina in winter. It is the Taormina that the tourists love, with the morning rain and the sun shining among the clouds laying on the sea, dominated by the mass of the whitened volcano placed above the blue of the gulf of Naxos. The medieval town is the perfect starting point for trips by car in order to go in search of seafood gastronomy, secret flavours of the hinterland and extraordinary landscapes between the rivers and the volcano.

There are two sides to travel over, the first one follows the seaside street along the highway 114 towards Messina with a view on the Strait, the other one, on the opposite direction towards the Mount Etna that climbs up inside the winding valley dug by the river Alcantara.

From Taormina to Roccalumera

Walk down towards Mazzarò by taking via Pirandello without losing sight of the Isola Bella stretched out on the sea, then go on towards Spisone along via Nazionale. The first gastronomic stopover is the restaurant La Capinera of Piero d'Agostino (Tel. 0942626247), young chef from Messina riding on the crest of a wave. This restaurant, also recommended by the French guidebook

On the left, the coast and the hotels on the sea of Letojanni.
Next to it Taoarte, some projections of the Old Theatre.
Below, corso Umberto and its shops, boutiques and art houses

of the young European restaurant managers, has a simple but sophisticated terrace on the sea. It suggests a very accurate traditional but revised cooking, from the homemade bread to the sesame and the chocolate. If you have the chance to talk to the chef, he will underline all the work behind every dish, even the simplest ones like the tuna fish, the swordfish and the grouper cut and served uncooked, and the bread baked in several versions, served hot from the oven and seasoned with olive oil.
Driving towards Letojanni, the crossroads is 6 kilometres away; among the houses you can see the beautiful beach of fine sand, desert in winter. If you want to taste the new seafood cuisine, go to Nino's (Tel. 0942651060) that in March opens the big veranda on the beach. You can also choose the restaurant Agrodolce on the left, at the end of the promenade. The cooking is all made with fish, meat or local vegetables. You cannot miss the real triumphs of the sea, served on ceramic plates, coloured with blue, yellow, green and purple pastel shades, made at the laboratory of Caleca di Patti.
Drive back on the highway going in the direction of Capo S. Alessio; the road follows the coast and shows the ruins of the castle. Look at the panoramic view with its typical urban chaos of the two coasts between

EVENTS YOU CANNOT MISS

Taoarte

Everything starts from the ancient theatre of Taormina, from those red stones that are mirrored in the Ionian Sea and soften under the magic of the big volcano. In this magical scenery the curtain rises and you can see the international art: music, theatre, cinema, photography and dancing. Here, from June to October, everything is of the outmost importance; there are world premieres, exhibitions, theme sections, festivals, competitions and guests from all over the world, on and off the stage. If you want to spend an unforgettable night, stay under the moon in the theatre terraces; for meetings, go to the several hotels, terraces, restaurants, and visit the alleys of the old town. The Sicilian country town, loved by the international tourism, becomes a set suitable for everyone: the big masters of the art, multi-awarded authors and actors, career artists, talented young people and a more and more crowded and interested audience.

Taormina Arte Foundation
Address: corso Umberto and Palazzo dei Congressi
Tel. 094221142
Opening: 8.30, 2-4 p.m., 7 p.m.
Website: www.taormina-arte.com

TAORMINA, THE LUXURY QUEEN LOOKING FOR HIDDEN LOCATIONS

Starting from June, the core of Taormina throbs around the theatre. In the morning, take a walk in corso Umberto that at night is swarming with tourists. Once you get past the Porta dell'Orologio, the medieval part of the city starts from Porta Messina and arrives to Porta Catania. Corso Umberto with the facades of the old buildings and the aristocratic balconies, with the daylight seems to be less crowded than in the afternoon, when it is illuminated by the signs and the shops. Make a stopover to the green area of the city residence that shows rare tropical species.
Walk along the promenade IX Aprile, to see the deconsecrated church of S. Agostino, built at the end of the 15th century; it has a monastery, the city library and the big reading rooms with frescoed ceilings; it is perfect if you want to have a break and look about magazines and old manuscripts.
In piazza Duomo, you can visit the apse and the 16th-century Sicilian marble statues inside the church. There are also valuable works of art like the polyptych "Last Supper" by Antonello da Messina and other 16th-century paintings. For those who love the ancient art, very interesting is the sacristy with the huge wooden wall-hung piece of furniture and, in the last room, the treasure of silverwares and vestments.
Go back towards the ancient theatre, in the direction of via B. Croce and make a tempting stop to the Bam Bar that in summer prepares at least 18 different tastes of fruit crushed-ice drinks. Excellent is the one made with

Sicily and Calabria, covered by the concrete. You can notice that this strip of sea between Sicily and Cariddi once was a place of extraordinary beauty. Once you get to Capo, leave the car and walk around the fortress leaning out over the transparent sea: on the blue sea on the right there is Capo Taormina while on the left you can see the Strait.
From here, make a 6 kilometres detour via the small village Forza d'Agrò. It is a medieval terrace stretching out between the sea and the mountains. Visit the arch Durazzesco, the 16th century church with big blue wooden altars and the statues of the Saints. The Saracen castle dominates from above the built-up area and a small quite square where you can sit and enjoy the winter sun. Along via dell'Annunziata, a small bar prepares at lunchtime unforgettable baked arancine, rice balls filled with ragout made of mixed and chopped meat.
Those who love silence and the rarefied air of the small mountain villages, can spend the night in the Bouganville (Tel. 0942721115), a beautiful and cheap B&B situated in the medieval area, few steps away from the castle. The owner will serve to the guests tasty apricot and peach marmalades made with the fruit that she picks up from her farmland in the promenade "l'Arburazzu".
Go back again towards the highway, leave behind the chaotic town of S. Alessio and after 7/8 kilometres you will get to another charming oasis. It is the small village Savoca, situated on a rocky ridge between sea and woods. Undamaged is its Norman style with the stone facades of the 16th-century buildings. Also intact are the 17 churches and the panoramic view at an altitude of 300 metres open wide on the Etna.
As a matter of fact, at the beginning of the 70s, Savoca was chosen

figs, as well as peach, watermelon and the typical almond.
In Taormina there are the most beautiful hotels of the island. The quality of the hospitality and the position are just unrivalled. It is hard to say which one is the best luxury old structure. However, the one the tourists love the most is S. Domenico Palace, while the newest is the charming hotel Villa Taormina, loved especially by French people. In the old town, other 5 stars luxury hotels are about to open. Even if it is a holiday place, the city offers several restaurants. For instance, behind the hall of Palazzo S. Stefano with its 14th-century restored tower that can be visited from early in the morning to 7 p.m., there is a secluded inn called Osteria Nero d'Avola (Tel. 0942628874); there, you can drink Sicilian wines combined with salads or a wide range of local cheeses and salami, from the rare Piacentino cheese to the salami coming from the Nebrodi.
At dusk, during the cinema festival, all the VIPs move to the Grand Hotel Timeo, right under the hall of the theatre for the usual press conference and the photographers. For dinner, after the shows, the favourites stay in Casa Grugno in vicolo S. Maria dei Greci (Tel. 094221208), where the chef prepares 3 special menus. They also go to La Baronessa restaurant (Tel. 0942620163) in the main street, in the internal super-panoramic room or in the open-air terrace during summer. The most typical restaurant loved by the stars is La Botte (Tel. 094224198) open also after midnight.

Taormina, the Badia Vecchia and the Etna in the background

by Francis Ford Coppola for some scenes of The Godfather part II. From then on, the sign of the bar Vitelli, at the entrance of the town, has been very popular. Savoca is a destination for few tourists that love sitting at a bar that recalls the 50s, enjoying the good old days atmosphere and talking to Mrs. Maria that still remembers the cast of the American directors. Even Al Pacino left her an autograph and a picture. Today this bar has become a small and weird bazaar selling local products such as the homemade limoncello and tasteless souvenirs like ceramic and lava items.
Leave Savoca and, after about ten kilometres of inland streets, get to the highway leading at the town of Roccapalumera. Get past the houses and, on the left, surrounded by a sea of citrus fruits, make a detour via the small village of Allume, the name remembers the alum, a potassium mineral having a cicatrizant property that used to be extracted from the mines of the area. There are just few houses that at Christmastime look like a lovely crib of craftsmen and farmers, a torrent and the small country restaurant Conte d'Antares (Tel. 0942746206) that has been there for at least 20 years. The specialties are always the same: the exclusive homemade pasta with wild boar ragout or the ravioli filled with orange.

From Taormina to Castiglione di Sicilia

Once you get past the bay of Giardini Naxos, that in summer becomes a quite crowded holiday place, take the ring road under the motorway and

SPEND THE NIGHT IN LUXURY HOTELS

Grand Hotel Timeo
Address: via Teatro Greco 59
Tel. 094223801
Rates: double room from 189 to 400 euros

San Domenico Palace
Address: piazza S Domenico 5
Tel. 0942613111
Rates: double room from 350 to 600 euros

Atlantis Bay
Address: via Nazionale 161 - Mazzarò
Tel. 0942618011
Rates: double room from 362 to 440 euros

Villa Sant'Andrea Hotel
Address: via Nazionale - Mazzarò
Tel. 094223125
Rates: from 226 to 400 euros

Villa Angela
Address: via L. Da Vinci 41
Tel. 094227038
Rates: from 85 to 125 euros

Villa Ducale
Address: via L. Da Vinci 60
Tel. 094228153
Rates: double room 250 euros

Casa Cinzia
Address: via G. Verdi
Tel. 3393774568 - 3343283753
Rates: B&B from 100 euros

keep driving on the right, then follow the highway 148 towards Trappitello and Francavilla di Sicilia. This is the first natural gate of the valley of the river Alcantara.
After 15 kilometres, get past the built-up area of Gaggi, beyond the private entrance with the refreshment bar of the Gole dell'Alcantara, get in the core of the protected area. Alcantara is the fourth natural park of Sicily, the only big river basin that provides the area with water and energy.
Driving on the highway you will be surprised by the quantity of citrus and seasonal fruits showed in the wooden boxes on sale along the streets near the holiday farms. Make a detour on the right, down to the built-up area of Motta Camastra. At an altitude of 450 metres, you will see a wide panoramic terrace where you can enjoy the amazing valley and the volcano; it is a real picture especially at dusk. The seat of

A view of the valley of Alcantara. On the right the green of the Picciolo Golf Club of Castiglione di Sicilia

the park and the information bureau is in Francavilla di Sicilia (Tel. 0942989911). From here, those who want to walk through rivers and woods can start from the comfortable Sentiero delle Gurge, one kilometre away. Five more kilometres and, once you get past the bridge of S. Nicola, enter in the province of Catania. On the left, it is worth it to go up until you get to the medieval built-up area of Castiglione di Sicilia. Make a stop at the square Dispensa dell'Etna, there is a lovely wine bar with a kitchen and an indoor terrace with a view on the Cathedral. Taste and, if you want, buy the renowned red wines of the Etna or the pecorino cheese, the pi-

A view of the valley of Alcantara. Above, the rafting on the river

stachio, the hazelnuts and the hot pepper in handy vacuum-packed boxes. You can also buy the homemade preserves of dried tomatoes and the exquisite citrus marmalades (Tel. 0942984258). From Castiglione you can still go up until the crossroads of Cerro, then turn on the right towards Randazzo until you see the first road signs that bring to the golf course Il Picciolo. It is the only golf course of Sicily having 18 holes; you can stop there for the night in a rural and comfortable guest flat in order to enjoy a whole day at the golf course.

On your way back to Taormina, drive along the road Randazzo-Fiumefreddo and after about 11 kilometres go down to the bridge of the river Alcantara towards the beautiful beach of Fiumefreddo, recently awarded by the blue flags of the European Union. ■

GOLF CLUB
IL PICCIOLO

The first golf course that Sicily can be proud of, was built in 1989, according to the plan of the architect Luigi Rota Caremoli. It has 18 holes squeezing through oak trees, hazels and rows of vineyards. The main character of the golf course is Mount Etna (3.340 metres).
From Fiumefreddo di Sicilia, drive along the highway 120 towards Randazzo. Once you get past Linguaglossa, after about 800 metres beyond the crossroads for Castiglione di Sicilia, you will get to the Golf Club.
We are at an altitude of 650 metres on the sea level. The course winds around the spectacular landscape with orchards and vineyards in the background: 18 holes, 72 par, and 5870 metres. The guestroom has 13 rooms, 5 of them on the first floor and 8 in a mansard roof. The restaurant, built in the old millstone of the ancient manor house has now turned into an elegant and sophisticated Club House; it offers traditional local dishes as well as typical Mediterranean specialties. The restaurant is open also for dinner only under reservation. Closed on non-holiday Tuesdays.

Il Picciolo Golf Club
Address: via Picciolo - Castiglione di Sicilia (CT)
Tel. 0942986252
Website: www.ilpicciologolf.com

The spectacular formation of lava rocks along the river Alcantara

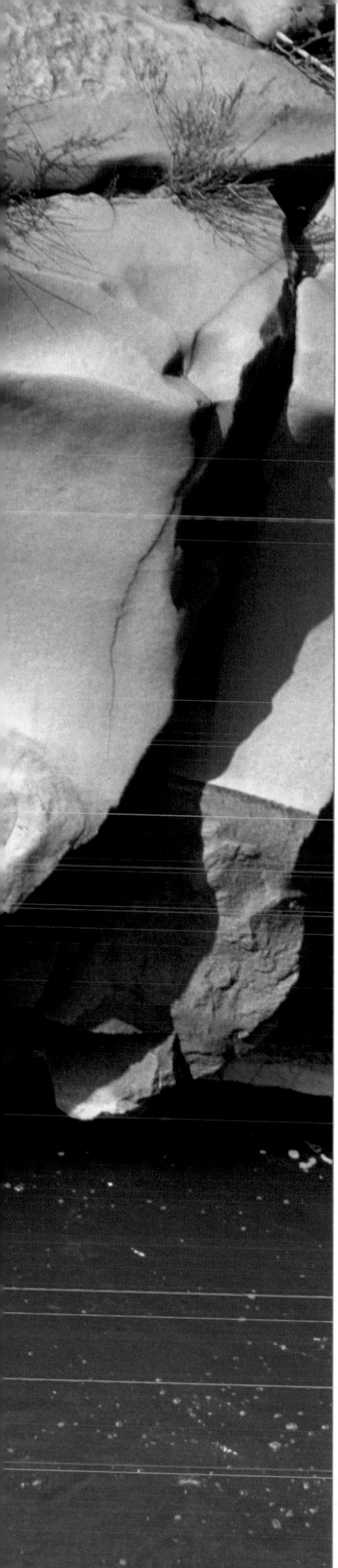

IN THE RIVER PARK OF **ALCANTARA**

The Alcantara, is a natural system of almost primitive beauty. Here, the landscape is shaped on the contact between water and fire. From the sea of Giardini Naxos to kilometres and kilometres of valleys, you can admire the big natural architectures: gorges, smooth walls, waterfalls, blocks of smooth and squared stones like they were carved by men.

The river basin is one of the most important things of the island because of the strong flow coming from the Nebrodi; it never runs aground. The lava and the volcanic eruption, the river, now swollen now clear, the vegetation, the citrus orchards, the vegetable gardens, the rural houses and the old shabby railway. This park recalls the local architecture characterized by the dark stones of the rural villages that open up on the river, it is surrounded by citrus orchards and vegetable gardens and by a nature that in spring exhales plenty of perfumes: Spanish brooms, orchids, oleander, etc. The river vegetation with its Oriental plane tree, the white willow and the Salix Gussonei, has endemic species that mingle with citrus fruits, prickly pears and orchards along the shores at few metres from the water.

Nowadays, there are 11 built-up areas: Francavilla with an archaeological site of inestimable value, a settlement of the Greek age where the open-cut mining is in progress and a museum that shows the discovered finds; Castiglione di Sicilia, the city of the red wine that has a visiting centre open for students and tourists and Motta Camastra, small ancient village that looks like a high and lonely crib.

In order to enjoy the river, today it is possible to walk up the falls with booths and swimsuit starting from the Gole di Larderia where you can rent the necessary equipment. It is a private entrance that during summer is stormed by tourists; there is also a lift that brings you to the natural pools without getting tired. If you want to find alternative entrances, follow the directions of the guides of the park.

If you want to admire the river and the unrivalled beauty of its water splashes and lava rocks, the best season is between May and June. You can walk along the paths that skirt the shores or go by jeep or mountain bike. The sportspeople can walk up the river with an appropriate equipment, but be careful to the current and the eddies near the electric power points.

Website: www.alcantara.it
Tel. 0942989911
Randazzo visiting centre
Tel. 095790001

SPEND THE NIGHT

S. Marco Castle
Address: via San Marco 40 - Calatabiano (CT)
Tel. 095641181
Rates: B&B from 55 euros

Il Borgo firm
Address: provincial road 32 - Frazione Mitogio (ME)
Tel. 0942985010
Rates: double room in B&B 60 euros

MESSINA

If you say Messina you mean the Strait. Actually, the city is placed between the coast and the hills; it overlooks the blue and deep sea that made his history from Scilla to Cariddi. However, bridge yes or bridge no, the city is anyway in an enclosed quite area still bound up with the customs and the flavours of the old good days. Razed by the seaquake at the beginning of the century, Messina was rebuilt following the traces of the Liberty style: from the facades of the buildings to the rail fences, even the building of the custom house, the recently restored Vittorio Emanuele Gallery and the new and comfortable Grand Hotel Liberty (Tel. 0906409436) at few steps from the station and the promenade. Around the square Cairoli and the historic bars Billé and Irrera the happy hour is constantly arranged, as well as the coffee and whipped cream water ice, the popular "menza ca' panna" or the huge brioches with the several fruity tastes.

Messina is also the city of the art treasures shown in the regional museum (Tel. 090361292) not really popular for the inhabitants of Messina. The museum, situated along the promenade, is inside a building that once was an old spinning mill; it still has a patio with a well in the middle and the tropical plants. In springs, among flowers and perfumes, there are live concerts. Well-organized are the first big rooms dedicated to the paintings of the Flemish period, as well as the paintings by Caravaggio and his school; they all are masterpieces of the 17th-century Sicilian paintings made by great authors. Actually, Caravaggio had lived and worked there for a year during his escape. Upstairs, there is the 18th-century silver Manta, impressive bas-relief that shows the mantle of the Virgin; it is a wonderful masterpiece of goldsmith's art influenced by the Byzantine and Oriental art. Another masterpiece is the big gold mantle kept in the treasure area of the Cathedral.

Messina has small high-quality pubs and typical small restaurants where you can taste the local dishes; the most popular is the stockfish salad in a dripping pan or the dried codfish marinated with celery, onion and other ingredients. Do not miss the swordfish rolls at the small restaurant Sascha, (Tel. 0902922950), very good at cooking homemade pasta seasoned with fish and lobster. Go to the Durlindana restaurant (Tel. 0906413156), it is one of the few open-air yards where you can have lunch away from the traffic and surrounded by the perfume of the lemons; they serve fresh fish and exquisite Sicilian desserts such as the cassata with ricotta cheese, the chocolate soufflé, the almond biscuits and the Passito wine from Pantelleria. More sophisticated is the cuisine of Vivaldi, the trendy restaurant that has

few tables and is situated at few steps from the lyric theatre. The specialty is the swordfish caponata, the "carbonara", homemade pasta made with smoked tuna fish, or the citrus fruit jelly. The newest restaurant is the Macellaio (Tel. 090719385); thanks to the exquisite fish dishes, it has become, in a flash, a busy meeting place as an alternative to the other restaurants. It is in the central via S. Giacomo right next to the Dome; the specialties are the meat cooked in front of the clients, the rolls and the tasteful pork chops wrapped in the bacon; simple but very effective side dishes. The tradition of the jewels, the gold-working and the stone-cutting is not lost in this city, there are still surprising designers and craftsmen that carve wood and work leather. For instance, there is Sansone, a new firm started up for a family passion that now produces small nice souvenirs and boxes containing the pictures of the palisade of the city before it was destroyed.
Going towards Ganzirri, popular for the production of small but tasty mussels, make a stop to Capo Faro and the small village. Here, you can find the last fishermen of swordfish that still today, in the waters of the Strait between Sicily and Cariddi, keep alive the old tradition of the fishing on the feluccas. ■

FISHING THE SWORDFISH

They are the last feluccas of the small village Ganzirri that overlooks the Strait under Capo Faro. Recently gathered in an association, the fishermen started doing the fishing for tourists in order to continue the millennial tradition of the swordfish hunting. Put out to sea all day long, in July or August, time and place have to be arranged with the fishermen or the Necton association (Tel. 090391646) near the Horcynus Orca park (Tel. 090325236).
The feluccas are big wooden sailing or motor boats with the typical sighting tower useful to spot the swordfish in the waters between Scilla and Cariddi. Like centuries ago, the fish is harpooned and loaded on board. Those who love the sea life will feel an unforgettable emotion.

The harbour of Messina and a panoramic view of the Strait, on the left the Cathedral

CATANIA

Every moment is the right one: autumn, winter and especially summer. The good season changes the look of the streets that wind up towards the old town where Giovanni Verga and Vincenzo Bellini used to live. Right from the obelisk of the elephant, symbol of the city placed in piazza Duomo, you should start your trip that has been already tried by dozens of thousands of young people. Via Etnea, recently restored with lava stones and artistic lighting, will make your night walk special. In Catania, you can find everything you need, from the itineraries of the baroque style along via Etnea and via dei Crociferi to the fish or antique markets. Those who love jazz music can go to the pub Il Pantagruele, for those who love metal music instead, there is an entire district, the one that surrounds piazza Teatro Massimo. Try a "shortino", a drink made of rum with a slice of lemon on the top of the glass, cane sugar soaked in absolute alcohol and then lighted: it is the so called "Torch", a drink that lays down the law of the alternative places of the nigh life in Catania. You can try it in the busy pub "Le Torce" full of motorcyclists, heavy-metal freaks but also people who

On the left, Piazza Duomo.
Below, the Cathedral, a panoramic view of the centre of Catania end its harbour.
Above, the bust of St. Agata

THE FESTIVAL OF **ST. AGATA**

The first week of February is dedicated to the celebration of the Patroness S. Agata. The believers with their white "bag", parade through the streets of the city centre carrying heavy candles (up to 70 kilos) on their back as sign of devoutness. They walk for dozens of kilometres with the burning flames of the candles. Next to them there are always the "candelore" big and lighted altars that represent the life of S. Agata, they weigh at least 800 kilos and are carried by butchers, fishmongers and farmers, divided by their jobs.

CATANIA

A MUSEUM YOU CANNOT MISS

Ursino Castle

The museum dates back between 1239 and 1250. It is situated inside the castle built in the Frederick's age and has a big yard. The rebuilding of the late 16th century is pretty obvious, especially in the Gothic-Catalan portal inside the chapel of S. Giorgio. At the end of the 90s, a whole restoration has given to the city the fortress-museum. The collections include several archaeological finds, vestments, valuable miniatures, engravings and masterpieces belonging to the Middle Ages and the Renaissance. A great part of the shown items come from the private collections of the prince Biscari and the Benedictine princes. Some Greek-Roman finds belong to the Biscari's collection as well as some pots of the old Camarina. Very valuable is the picture gallery with some masterpieces that date back to the beginning of the 15th century until the 19th century. Among the others, the Last Judgment by Beato Angelico is the one that shines.

Address: piazza Federico di Svevia
Tel. 095345830
Opening: from Mon to Sat 9 a.m. to 1 p.m., closed on Sunday

love "particular" places. In the district of via Landolina you can do the shopping at night, between a shortino and a bier you have to "pop over" to Freak, it sells gifts and fancy goods, vintage and ethnic clothing, and strictly handcrafted leather clothes. If you move to the Irish-pub, you can breath the typical Irish atmosphere surrounded by malt beer and live music every night. However, the real place throbbing with life is via Plebiscito, where the perfumes floating on air remove every doubt: horse meat, "cipollate" (onions) with pork and sausages and the red wine of the Etna. Those who love the soft lights have to go to Tabacco for a happy hour, it is right in front of the city hall.

If you want to spend the night, go to the B&B Pantagruele in the city centre. Downstairs, there is a wine bar that also sells local salami and pork meat (Tel. 3284087368). If you want to stay in the city centre, go to the comfortable Katane hotel with its renowned restaurant Il Cuciniere (Tel. 0957470702). On the seaside towards Acireale, there is the Baia Verde hotel (Tel. 095491522) and the Sheraton Catania (Tel. 0957114111), both have rooms with a view on the lava cliff and on the blue sea.

The restaurant that moves up the table is "Karol" run by Carlo Piazza in via Cagliari behind viale Vittorio Veneto; on the list only fish and ten different appetizers (marinated fish, fried mixed fish, mussels au gratin, farmhouse mushrooms, etc). Two main courses and a second course will cost you 30 euros, drinks included (Tel. 3394400818).

Acireale, Piazza Duomo

Catania, outside the city walls

If the inhabitants of Catania want to take a trip, they go in places that are only 10 kilometres away from Catania: Acireale, Aci Castello, Acitrezza, Isola dei Ciclopi, the protected marine area, and the sea village Santa Maria La Scala.

A must see is Acireale, with its beautiful square, the 16th-century baroque Dome but also the renowned historical pastry shop ex Costarelli, where you can buy the Sicilian marzipan and the sweets with pistachio. Another sanctuary of sweets, crushed-ice drinks and ice creams is the pastry shop Castorina in corso Savoia.

Make a stop to Aci Castello and visit the lava stone Norman castle situated on the top of the rocks. 2 kilometres later there is Acitrezza with its beautiful small harbour and the equipped beach lido dei Ciclopi.

Very impressive are the basalt rocks coming out of the blue sea; the island of Aci also has a marine biology institute. Make the last gastronomic stopover to Santa Maria La Scala, a fishermen's village between the green of the citrus orchards and the coast. On the promenade you can have a meal in one of the several small restaurants. They cook fresh fish and the unmissable local "mascolini", white anchovies marinated with lemon, typical dish of the Etna coast. ■

On the right, the fountain of the Amenano in Catania. Below, Acitrezza, the stacks and the islands of Lachea

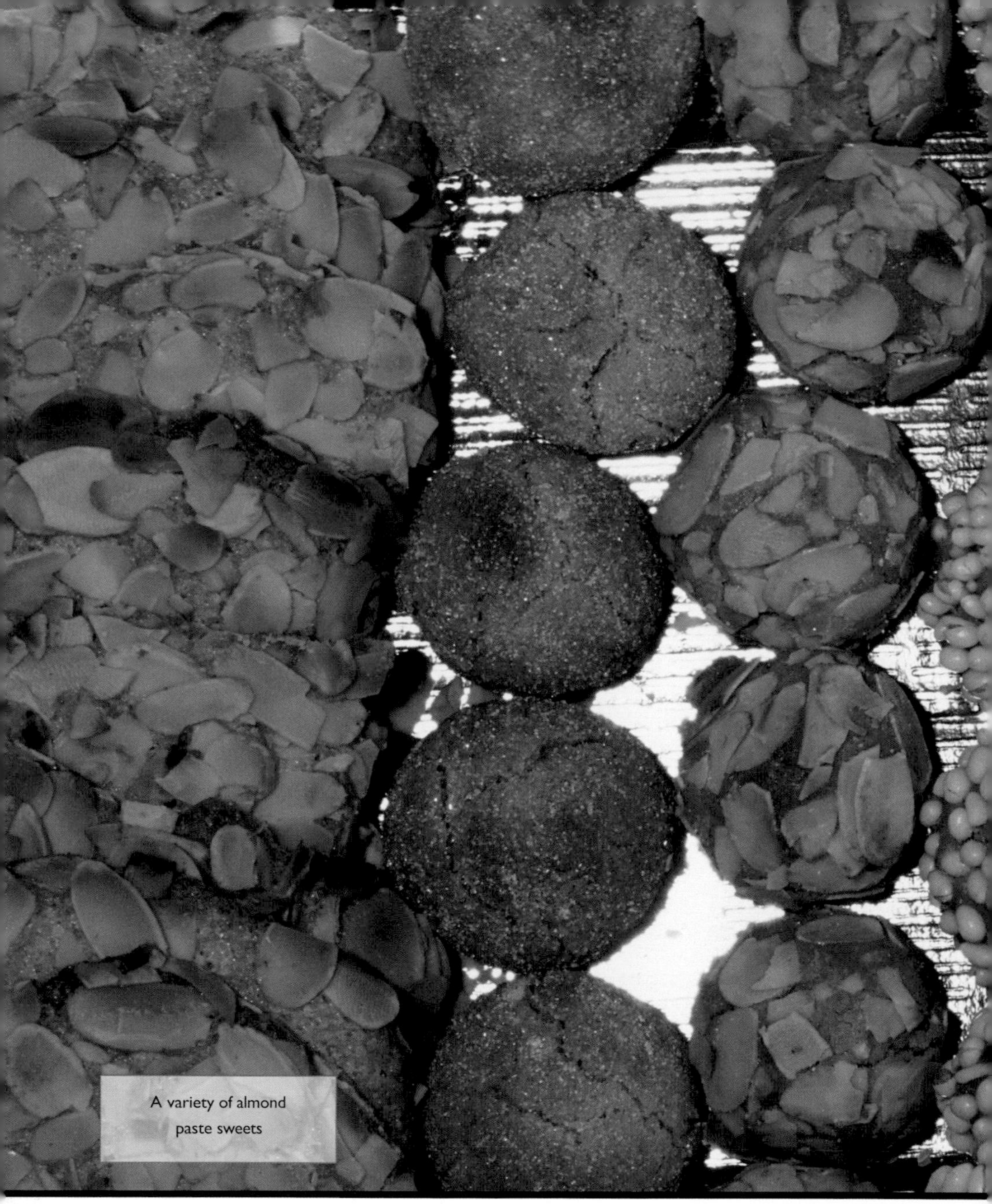

A variety of almond paste sweets

10

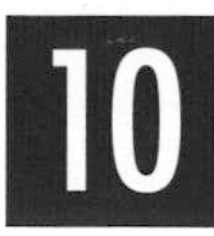

SICILIAN FLAVOURS
A TASTEFUL JOURNEY

Go in search of the lost flavours by tasting the local products.
Province after province, discover the itinerary that goes from nature to taste, from traditions to renewals, from history to future, under the protective wing of the Slow Food association

Palermo and surroundings, from the street food to the mountain flavours

Palermo is the starting point, exactly from those historic markets described before; take a walk there surrounded by the scents, the sounds and the flavours of the tradition. Start from the street kitchens often turned into stalls or respectable fried-food shops selling plenty of popular street food: "panelle" (fritters made with chickpea flour), mashed potatoes croquettes, fried aubergines, bread with beef spleen and ricotta cheese, beef or pork "stigghiole", boiled and seasoned entrails (from the cartilage to knees or other parts of the animal), octopus, snails, potatoes, French beans, boiled artichokes, onions, aubergines and roast peppers. Go on and admire the "fruits' altars": dried fruits, seasoned olives, citrus fruits, seasonal specialties, local vegetables but also cantaloupes and watermelons. Among the citrus fruits do not miss the late mandarins from Ciaculli, few seeds, thin peel, very sweet, they grow in the last terraced gardens now protected from the concrete in the few fields of the Conca d'oro association.

Go up for few kilometres towards the hills that frame the city. There, from Cinisi to Godrano, among sunny knolls and panoramic woods,

you will find herds of surviving cows, especially the black ones from Cinisi, able to produce a very nourishing and aromatic milk used to make an old and very appreciated cheese, the "caciocavallo", considered as the Sicilian parmesan. Always up to the hills, above the Imera valley, you can meet the king of the vegetables that has a reign of hectares and hectares: the artichoke from Cerda that here is particularly sweet and pulpy. A monument in the main square, a spring festival and even a book with more than a hundred recipes are dedicated to the artichoke, you will never get sick of having it. Go now towards the Madonie Park, the first village is Scillato also called the garden town. With its several mills, Scillato welcomes the wonderful orchards of oranges and apricots. A little bit higher is Polizzi Generosa with its churches, convents, aristocratic buildings and two gems that you cannot miss: the "badda" bean (that means ball) and the "sfoglio". The badda bean has been cultivated for centuries in the mountain orchards, it is small, two-coloured and scented, you can eat it fresh or dried, both with vegetables and meat. The secret recipe of the sweet sfoglio was invented 500 years ago by the Bene-

In the top, the Sicilian marzipan fruits. In the picture below, some typical caciotta cheese from the Madonie

dictine nuns and then handed down with pride. It is made with fresh cheese, short pastry, candied fruit, cinnamon, eggs and chocolate. You can eat it after one month and is always delicious. Now the road takes to the central massifs of the Park. There, the shepherds and the several dairies produce, also live, the popular "provola" (round-shaped soft cheese made from buffalo milk). Do not miss the hot ricotta cheese spread on local bread. These are also the woods of the mythical manna, which nowadays is cultivated only by the ash trees of Pollina and Castelbuono. Decongestant and laxative, the manna is a natural sweetener that, with the past of the years, has become pleasant news for the confectionery industry, it also used iced with the panettone (spiced brioche with sultanas), the Easter cake and the Sicilian marzipan.
There's no accounting for taste: Ustica is famous for the tender and tasty lentils, the smallest of Italy.

Trapani, the countryside in a sea of flavours

The streets that take to the Trapani valleys, going through green vineyards, beaches and blue small inlets, in summer turn into a tidy carpet with yellow and green spots. It deals with the endless cultivation of melons considered as works of art in the fine quality of the yellow Cartucciaro di Paceco and the green Purceddu di Alcamo.
They are also called winter melons, sweet and juicy. Once, they were kept

In the top on the left an olive grove near Trapani. Below, the manna taken from the ash tree of the Madonie

in the cellar, then hanging on a balcony, and were only eaten for the Christmas night until February. Today, the ice-cream sellers also use them to prepare exquisite crushed-ice drinks. The streets now take to Segesta where its extraordinary tracks bring to the sea having the Aegadian Islands as a background. Before you leave, do not miss the medieval village Erice. Visit the castle, the small churches, the stone houses, the romantic streets and the perfumed pastry shops specialized in preparing soft sweets and almond biscuits to eat together with the homemade brownings seasoned with citrus fruits, bay leaves and cinnamon. Now go towards the islands in order to take a sunbath, a swim and a "flavour bath". Try the strong and expert flavours that you can find in the original old swordfish botargo in Favignana; it is produced by the last small craft business that works the fish, not only the tuna fish, in the old way of the expert salters of the Florio family, that wanted to create their loved and huge tunny-fishing area right there.
Now go back to the mainland city along the Phoenician coast and admire the red dusk, lying on the saltpans of Trapani, which gracefully stretches over the Mozia Island, down to Marsala and above its cellars and vineyards with a warm ray of 180 degrees.

Below, a blossom almond grove.
On the right a detail
of the Sicilian cassata

Here you can find the districts of the quality sierras that generate a niche product precious in the kitchen and useful for your health: the red garlic from Nubia; it is very intense and rich in allicin. Go down towards Castelvetrano and you will understand what really is the so popular rye bread. It is round shaped and has a crunchy crust sprinkled with sesame seeds, soft yellow paste, baked only inside wood-burning ovens, this bread, the only one in Sicily, is so good because of the old variety of wheat that makes it sweeter. Eat it hot from the oven, or lukewarm, or cold, or even dried with some tomatoes and a slice of Vastedda del Belice, the only goat's milk cheese produced by the dairymen in summer. When the olives of these valleys begin to ripen, they become green and big and are used to produce the most awarded PDO olive oil.

There is also another island in the surroundings that is worth to visit, that is Pantelleria. Enjoy the island by going around the "dammusi", the funerary buildings, the natural heaters, the hot waters, the Arab orchards, the Zibibbo vineyards, the Passito wine and the capers that grow up on beautiful and irresistible plants like its fruits. They are perfumed and taste like sea and land.

Agrigento, where the gods bless fruit and cheese

Go visit the magnificent Valle dei Tempi (valley of the temples), the Sicilian mountains and the luxuriant vineyards with fruits and vegetables that characterize the territory. On the right there is the sea, the beaches with the dunes and the plentiful and excellent fish that comes from the nets of the historic marine of Sciacca. Make a stop here plunged between history and taste. Start from two particular kinds of cheese: the "fiore sicano" and the "tuma persa", they have an ancient processing; the first one is made between caves and calcareous stones in order to ease the mildew, the second one produced with time and skill. They have a unique sweet and hot taste that is perfect if combined with olive oil and seasoned olives, only here people do that.
In this Pirandellian land of the big contradictions, the surprises go on with the strawberries from Ribera. Since the big war, they were perfectly naturalized at the feet of the lemon, orange and peach trees, until a group of veterans didn't want to renounce at the strawberry plants discovered in the north woods. Excellent in April and May, they are used to prepare cakes and fine ice creams all year long. Also try the renowned peaches of Bivona, the so-

In the top on the left and below the harvest of the prickly pears. In the top on the right a sheepfold and a rural house

called "montagnole". They are sunny, pulpy, and perfumed like nothing else; they brighten the Sicilian mountain slopes of the Plantani valley. Following the tradition of the quality, in Santa Maria del Belice there is a horizon characterized by the thick rows of prickly pears exported all over Europe. Try them fresh, or even icy with some bread. The grape harvesters used to have them for breakfast, served by the landlords to the workers in order to speed up the harvesting. Today, the prickly pear is the perfect dessert for autumn meals.

Caltanissetta and Enna, the places of the traditional taste

Go back to the core of Sicily, passing through streets and lanes that brush endless fields of wheat, olive groves, beautiful farms, reforestations, big sheepfolds, collapsed or restored castles, and remains of old sulphur and salt mines. These are the big feuds. Sometimes it seems like the time has stopped around the 11th century and it feels good.

Here, even the flavours belong to the past. Your palates will remember the recipes of the ancestors especially if they involve the violet artichokes from Niscemi, the capital of the sweetest vegetable ever, celebrated with two days of festival and food-and-wine combinations.

Also good in this area is the manual production of the broad bean from

Leonforte. It is the main ingredient of the local cuisine and the cultivation method is the rotation of crops with the wheat. The broad bean goes well with the hot and spicy taste of the piacentino cheese from Enna, very tasty and yellow because of the saffron that gives the flavour. Dealing with old recipes and traditional flavours, it's worth mentioning the crown-shaped biscuits that, in Delia, during the Sicilian Vespers were donated to the ladies of the castles. They are still prepared with the same ingredients: durum wheat flour, eggs, sugar, lard, red wine, cinnamon and orange peels. They are called "cuddrireddra" from the Greek Kollura that means ring finger-shaped flat bread.

Here the brand of the caciocavallo cheese from Ragusa. Below the typical dry walls. On the right the harvest of the carobs

Ragusa, from the fields to the pasturage pleasures

Among the white rock tablelands, the countryside of Ragusa welcomes dry-stone walls among ancient almond, olive and carob trees but also

historic yards and cottages, free herds, and the triumphs of the baroque. It is a slow land, rich in flavours and suggestions both strong and sweet. It is a total seduction that starts from the big onion of Giarratana. It can weigh from 500 grams to two kilos and has a white and tasty pulp that can be eaten both raw with some olive oil, boiled, roasted or with a spoon carrying the exquisite broad beans from Modica. The cows have been pasturing in these mountains forever; they produce dense and perfumed milk used for the PDO Ragusano cheese ripened in fresh cellars and produced in the dairies. Someone calls it the Hyblean ingot. Another exquisite cheese is the Hyblean cascavaddu; it has a strong taste and is the protagonist of all the meals in the province.

Ragusa is also the home of the real chocolate from Modica; it is pure, dark and faithful to the Aztec recipes, and today is the world leader in the production. It is used for several dishes, also savoury dishes, and has become the most natural and pleasant drug of the local cuisine. You can also find it in the several recipes dedicated to the pork of Chiaramonte Gulfi. Every single part of the small or big pork is eaten, from the nails to the ears.

Siracusa, when the almonds meet the anchovies

I suggest an itinerary of one thousand ideas: we are in Syracuse, on the right there is the Ionian sea teeming with fish and on the left the big valleys growing fruits and almond trees. Here, people are really proud of the seafood cooking because every variety of fish can be perfectly combined with the products of the land: the tuna fish with onions, the dolphin-fish fried with vinegar, the several versions of the dripping pan, the shellfish and vegetable rolls, the lobster ragout and the anchovies seasoned with toasted breadcrumbs. Also very good are the meat dishes, to name a few there are the homemade sausages from Palazzolo and the wild boar salami from Buccheri.

In Noto, there are also three different kind of almond trees: roman, pizzuta d'Avola and fascionello. Dense and irregular taste, white pulp that keeps aromas and fats, they have a heady scent; for this reason, Syracuse is in ruthless competition with Turkey. Try the almonds combined with the excellent local honey that thanks to the Arabs made Syracuse an unrivalled pastry maker. From the nougats to the sweets, from the cassata to the crushed-ice drinks, here the taste is another story, you will never forget it.

The salami of S.Angelo, a gastronomic specialty of the Nebrodi. In the top some sweets made with pistachios from Bronte

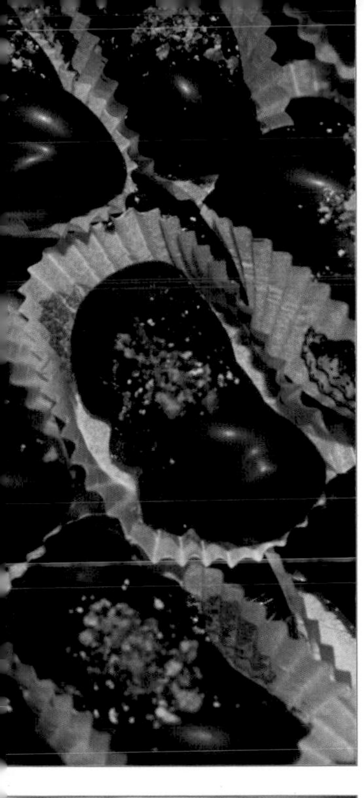

Catania, blood-orange looks well with the pistachio-green

The fishing has been practised since the Greek Homer. The fishermen lower the narrow-meshed nets and wait for the dawn to take them back. The heads of the anchovies get stuck in the net, the fish lose all the blood and, in this way, it is cleaner, tastier and finer. Nowadays, about 30 families still do the fishing in the Etnean coast that goes from Capo Mulini to Capo Santa Croce.
Let's now go back to the land under the big volcano that has turned the Catania plain into a real heaven of nature. Catania is the home of the blood oranges; they have an antioxidant property recognized by the medical science that recommends them. Catania is the land of the fruit; it is impossible to forget the peaches "tabacchiere" grown at the slopes of the Etna Mount. They have a flattened shape and are very scented, once they were the pride of the orchards for the farm workers and the noblemen and today they boast a good production and a modest export. This is another one-of-a-kind product that grows in the uneven European grounds.
His Majesty, the pistachio from Bronte, is green, shining, resinous, perfumed and more and more often used for desserts, pastries, ice-creams, creams and as dressing for every dish.

Messina, the island of salami, lemons and Malvasia wine

Let's now leave the Ionian coast in order to enter the woodland that characterizes the Nebrodi's Park; it is a park of flavours and landscapes. Here, a dense and exclusive cheese is made from herds of sheep and goats freely grazing in green pastures, it is the yellow "maiorchino" cheese, also the protagonist of a 17th-century game celebrated in the town of Novara, the main producer. The heavy shapes of the cheese are thrown by skilled shots down the steep streets for two kilometres. The winner is the one that can take the cheese to the end of the streets with the less number of shots. Same woods but different excellent cheese is the "provola" from the Nebrodi (round-shaped soft cheese made from buffalo milk). Try also the pasta with cheese ripened with lemon and the roasted ricotta cheese; or the pork grazing in these mountains, the renowned black pork from the Nebrodi, a frugal and not very common species. However, Messina is a great producer of salami (the best one is Sant'Angelo), sausages, pancetta and capocollo (another kind of sausage). Let's now go towards the luxury plains and the stone terraces that bring to the sea among thick citrus fruit orchards and old lemon groves from where the excellent "Interdonato" lemon shines. Once they were very popular in England and used with tea. On the opposite side you can see the Aeolian Islands, producers of the Malvasia, the sweet wine, nectar of the gods. ■

Pistachio ice-cream

Provincia Regionale
di Palermo

Giovanni Avanti

Palermo

A territory, a thousand of charming places. The districts of Palermo represent a crossroads of resources, colours, perfumes, a mosaic of history, art and gastronomy where the culture is a wonderful scene that constantly changes.
All the tourists that want to visit our country are not even spoilt for choice, because in one stay you can seize all the occasions: from the charming Norman site of Monreale to the beautiful several landscapes of the Madonie, from the architectural marvels of the chief town to the uncontaminated nature of Valle dello Jato, from the hinterland hallowed by the good Italian producers, to the "dolce vita" of the coast.
A territory, a thousand of shades, for a holiday that can last all year long.

Giovanni Avanti
President of Provincia Regionale di Palermo

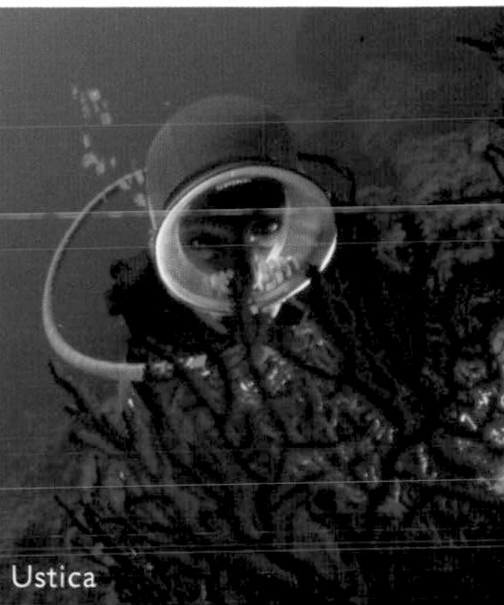

Ustica

Cefalù

Madonie